LUIS DE ZULUETA

*VELÁZQUEZ: "IT IS TRUTH, NOT PAINTING"*

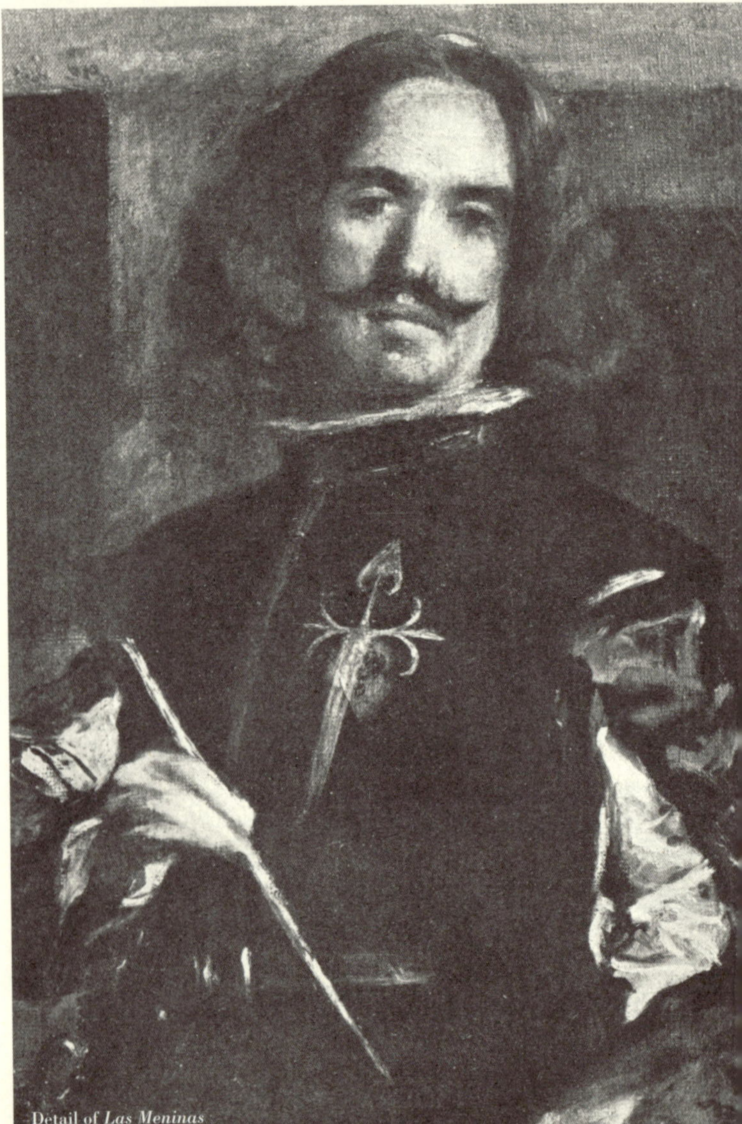

Detail of *Las Meninas*

LUIS DE ZULUETA

# Velázquez:

## "It is truth, not painting"

Translated by
Gillian Owtram de Zulueta

Publicaciones de la Residencia de Estudiantes

"Those of us who are neither researchers nor biographers, but observers, readers and from time to time, narrators." This is how the author of this new work on Velázquez describes himself. New as regards its publication, since its origin goes back to 1990, when the Prado Museum presented its magnificent Velázquez exhibition (from 23 January to 31 March). So strong was the impression it made on the author that, after it was over, he tells us that "Velázquez returned to life, or, more exactly, came into the world, the intricate world of communications which we suffer today, in that spring of 1990."

 ◆ DESIGN: MONTSE LAGO ◆ LAYOUT: JORGE JIMÉNEZ QUESADA ◆ PROOFREADING: BEATRIZ ANABITARTE ◆ COORDINATION OF THE PRESENT EDITION: RESIDENCIA DE ESTUDIANTES (TRILCE ARROYO) ◆ PRINTING: ARTES GRÁFICAS PALERMO ◆ BINDING: RAMOS ◆ ISBN: 84-95078-54-6 ◆ D. L.: M-817-2007 ◆ PRINTED IN SPAIN

# INDEX

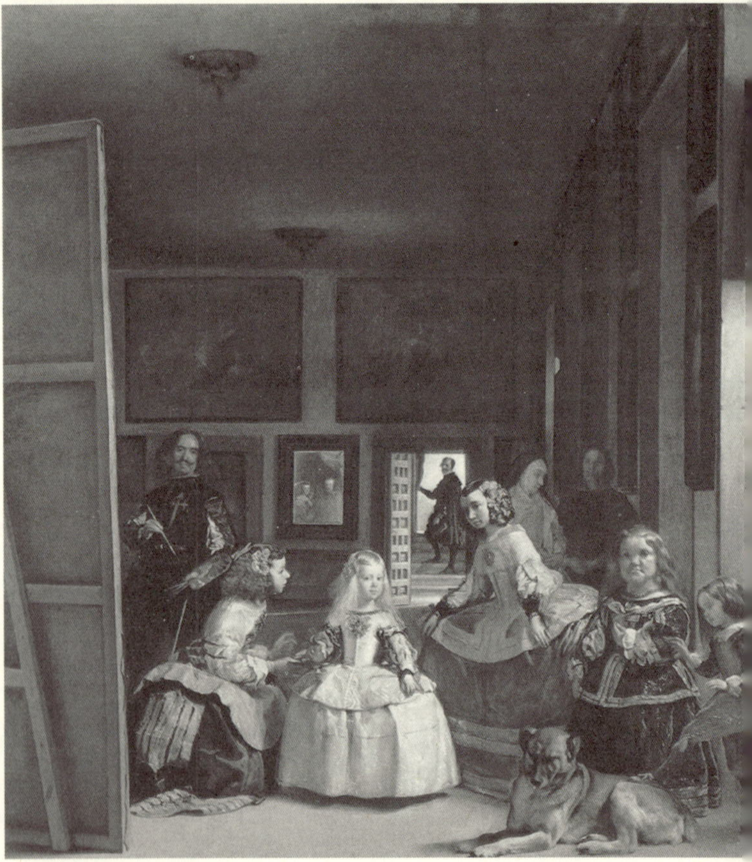

Diego Velázquez de Silva, *The Family of Philip IV* or "*Las Meninas*," 1656.
Oil on canvas, 3.18 x 2.76 m. (© Museo Nacional del Prado, Madrid)

## IN FRONT OF THE GREAT "TRUTH"

"Where is the picture?," Théophile Gautier is said to have exclaimed on finding himself for the first time in front of *Las Meninas*. Because he suddenly felt himself to be in the middle of the gallery "which is that of the prince which the picture shows and where it was painted." In fact, he had just entered the traditional setting of *Las Meninas* in the Prado, with its open balcony on the right and, slightly in shadow, the great picture at the end... He turned to his companions and saw himself in the mirror, placed in a corner of the room... Inside the picture! Yes, inside the picture, like one more personage there: "Théophile Gautier par Velázquez." Because the picture "is truth, not painting," as Palomino, Velázquez' first biographer, has said. The overpowering, bewildering impression given by *Las Meninas* cannot be better expressed than Palomino has done so concisely half a century after the picture was painted, and then Gautier, when a century and a half had passed since the melancholy end of the Austrian dynasty, the beginning of the end of the Spanish empire.

There is a hint of prophetic sadness in this "illustrious work of don Diego Velázquez" as Palomino describes *Las*

*Meninas*—the best picture in the world, according to Picasso—. "Don Diego Velázquez finished painting it in the year 1656." Palomino states; a date accepted by the numerous later biographers of Velázquez and confirmed by the latest and most exhaustive of them all, Jonathan Brown, in his monumental *Velázquez, Painter and Courtier*. 1656 was one of the most harrowing and melancholy years of Philip IV's reign. Thirteen years earlier, in 1643, the king, after a series of military and political disasters, had made his minister resign. He was the Count-Duke of Olivares, an Andalusian, like Velázquez, and had introduced him into the court. To celebrate his last military triumph, the battle of Fuenterrabía, Velázquez had immortalized him in a superb equestrian portrait. Three years after the fall of Olivares, in 1646, Prince Baltasar Carlos, the adolescent son and only male heir of Philip IV died unexpectedly in Saragossa, on a journey. He was the little equestrian and hunting prince of the Velázquez portraits, the reign's bright hope. His mother, Queen Isabella of Bourbon, had died only a short while before. The widowed king decided to remarry: The Spanish empire needed an heir. And, in 1649, he married his fourteen-year-old niece, Mariana of Austria (the promised bride of Baltasar Carlos). Barely two years later, on 12th July 1651, the firstborn of this unequal match was delivered with great difficulty—a girl! The enchanting Infanta Margarita. The young queen was seriously ill for a long time. The years passed and the wished-for heir did not come... In this sombre atmosphere of autumnal and courtly discouragement, in the gallery of the former quarters of the long mourned Prince Baltasar Carlos, *Las Meninas* were painted.

> Among the marvellous paintings which don Diego Velázquez did, writes Palomino, was the big picture with the portrait of the lady Empress (then infanta of Spain) doña Margarita María of Austria, at a very early age; there are no words to explain...

There were no words in 1656 to explain that "marvellous painting" and perhaps there are still none. To begin with, Palomino did not know how to define the painting, which did not conform to the usual norms of his time. And moreover, he did not think it was what was considered as "painting" in the 17th century—"it is truth, not painting," he has just told us emphatically—. But neither does he venture to call the enormous canvas "truth," as it is not "painting." And he describes it ambiguously, as we have just seen, as "the big picture with the portrait of the lady Empress." Because it is not really a "picture," like, for example, *The Surrender of Breda*, nor a "portrait," like that of the same lady Empress, at an even earlier age, raised up, all alone, on a platform covered by a big Oriental carpet, barely leaning against a table on which some roses in a transparent vase are beginning to shed their petals... The enormous canvas is something new, surprising. As surprising, as inexplicable—as scandalous—in the Madrid of 1656 as *Les Demoiselles d'Avignon* in the Paris of 1910.

But Palomino went on to say: "There are no words to express all her grace, vivacity and beauty; but her portrait itself is the best panegyric. Kneeling at her feet is doña María Agustina, an attendant to the queen, the daughter of don Diego Sarmiento, offering her water from a clay cup. On her other side is doña Isabel de Velasco (daughter of don Bernardino López de Ayala y Velasco, Count of Fuensalida, gentleman of His Majesty's bedchamber) attendant and afterwards Lady, with movement and action as though they would speak..." Movement and action stopped for an instant, for several centuries, as if in a cinematic "freeze." One has the impression, after some time in front of *Las Meninas*, or rather, inside *Las Meninas*, when one turns one's back on the motionless group to leave the imaginary gallery of the prince's room by the rear door, beside which the king and queen, had been standing, that the "freeze" ends and the great picture returns to movement and action: One hears the rustle of María Agustina's heavy silk farthingale as she rises to her feet with the cup which the capricious royal child has refused, though she had asked for it; doña Isabel de Velasco murmurs something, she was sure Her Royal Highness hadn't really wanted water, even if she had asked for it: The dog's great paws scratch the floor as he too gets up, with a grunt which may end in a hoarse bark of protest at little Nicolás

Pertusato, a dwarf, who keeps on treading on him—"to show how domesticated and docile he was in suffering, in spite of his ferocious aspect, because, while he was being painted, he stayed without moving where they had placed him"—, but there are limits to everything, after all, even for a dog... The formidable Mari Bárbola follows with her dull gaze someone who has turned his back and is leaving: His shadow, in jeans and vest, passes in a flash across the mirror, which had reflected the king and queen... Velázquez has disappeared again behind the canvas on which he is painting—a "picture," a "portrait," a "truth"? Behind, in the shadow, he has left his "tablet of colours" with a deep sigh of relief at feeling himself free from his forced, "frozen" immobility—he, who is a thinking meteor, hurled at unimaginable speed—three centuries in sixty years...! Isn't it this driving force—physical and mental—"frozen" in *Las Meninas,* which has put in motion the brilliant, infinite kaleidoscope of Picasso's "Las Meninas" series? Wasn't it Picasso's shadow which flashed across the mirror?

"This painting was highly esteemed by His Majesty, and while it was being done he frequently came to watch its painting... It was placed in His Majesty's downstairs quarters, in the room used as an office..." The private apartments, such as the king's office in the old Alcázar, had to be small, not much bigger than the room where *Las Meninas* traditionally hung in the Prado Museum. They were "spaces," as architects would say today, which could be warmed by a wood fire, sometimes only by a good brazier in the cold Madrid winters, when Madrid was cold and the fountains of the Prado froze and the wind from the Guadarrama whipped mercilessly round corners... In the limited space of the office, the great "truth," the "picture-portrait" of the little Margarita and her attendants, was hung on the bare wall at the end of the room, facing the entrance door. Slightly in shadow, the picture received its proper light, filtered through the bluish panes of the balcony on the right—exactly the same light in which it had been painted, almost the same light as that of Madrid today—. Because the canvas on which the picture, *Las Meninas*, was painted must in fact have faced in the opposite direction to the one on which Velázquez was "pretending" to paint. Two easels, back to back. But not directly behind each other. The two enormous canvases were placed diagonally in the gallery of the prince's quarters; the dummy canvas in the darkest part of the gallery, against the wall facing the balconies, so that the group around the infanta should have as much direct light as possible; and the canvas on which Velázquez was really painting the Prado's *Las Meninas*, at the other side of the gallery, further down than the dummy canvas, beside a last open balcony, also so as to be in the best possible light. For this reason, in *Las Meninas*, Velázquez is painting, absurdly, in the darkest part of the gallery, his improvised studio. A conscious absurdity: Velázquez, like the Cubists, changes the real order of the elements in his model to obtain a stronger, more characteristic image of that model, as they may place the two eyes on the same side of the nose. He also, according to his critics, Brown among others, alters the true perspective: The king and queen could not be reflected in the mirror, there is a distortion of the gallery's perspective... One sees what cannot be seen, perspective is altered; is this analytical pre-Cubism?

In the king's office, as in the Prado, there must have been a heavy Venetian mirror in the angle where the balcony wall joins the wall facing the picture, where the entrance door was probably placed, as it was in the room where *Las Meninas* used to hang in the Prado: On entering, a visitor would have felt overwhelmed, dazzled by the charming group which was occupying His Majesty's office... and moved hastily towards the door, murmuring excuses, turning his back on her serene Highness—five years old—doña Margarita María, infanta of Spain and, like Gautier, would have seen himself too in the mirror (inside the picture...) Because the mirror was placed behind the spot where Velázquez stood when he peered out from behind his canvas, with his "tablet of colours" and his brushes, to study the group he was painting. And so the intruder, who was in the same light and in line with the royal group in relation to the painter, would have seen himself reflected there too, in the little fragment of the picture bounded by the mirror's heavy ebony frame, inside the picture. The King, Philip IV, must often have felt himself, each day a little older and a lot more defeated, to be the centre of a world which was irremediably ending, "inside" that prophetic picture where, in the feigned mirror in the background, the image of the dynasty's last hope—the royal pair, a possible heir—grew every day more cold and faint.

A year, more or less, after the great "truth"—the implacable prophecy—was painted, on 28th November, 1657, the new heir, Prince Felipe Próspero, was born. The portents of gloomy ending which seem to float in the gallery of the lost prince's quarters disperse, are swept away... There remains only the implacable gaze of Velázquez, who wakes in the future and dreams in the past—the king's best friend, perhaps his only friend—; a steady, strong, deep look; unchanging. "At the other side, don Diego Velázquez is painting." According to Palomino's description, "he has the tablet of colours in his left hand, and in his right the brush; the key of the bedchamber and of *aposentador* at his waist and on his breast the Cross of Santiago which, after his death, His Majesty ordered to be painted; and some say that his Majesty painted it himself, to encourage the practitioners of this most noble art with such a superior chronicler, because when Velázquez painted this picture the king had not yet granted him this favour."

Jonathan Brown corrects the statement in his book *Velázquez, Painter and Courtier*: "Palomino claims that the king ordered the Cross of Santiago to be added to Velázquez' portrait after the death of the artist... It is impossible to test the validity of this statement without technical examination, and even then it might be a hopeless task because only four years had passed between the supposed date of completion and the death of the artist. Examination of the canvas after the recent cleaning (May-June 1984) seems to indicate that the brushwork of the Cross is uniform with the rest of the surface. If this is so, and Palomino is correct about the subsequent addition of the Cross, then this motif could have been added by Velázquez himself two or three years after the picture was painted." Those of us who are neither researchers nor biographers, but observers, readers and, from time to time, narrators, are tempted to go further than Palomino, but without disagreeing with Brown. The Cross of Santiago was bestowed on Velázquez a year after Felipe Próspero was born, exactly on the day of the prince's first birthday, 28th November 1658. The king then grants him the title of nobility and the order of Santiago receives him as a knight. Palomino tells us that the king had such a high regard for him personally "that he spoke to him more confidentially than as a king to his subject and discussed difficult business with him, especially in those more exclusive hours when the gentlemen and other courtiers had retired." It is easy to imagine that, during those "more exclusive hours" on the happy day of his heir's first birthday, the king might have called his bosom friend to come to his office; he has a great surprise for him. His Majesty asks him to bring his "tablet of colours" and some brushes. Velázquez enters the office with his palette and brushes. At the end of the room, in the semidarkness, the great "truth" palpitates arrhythmically with the luminous and uneven pulse of the wood fire. Without a word, the king, by the light of one of the silver candlesticks on his desk, mixes on the palette a vibrant red; with brush in hand, he approaches the great canvas at the end of the room and traces on Velázquez' black doublet a flat, inexpert cross, lacking relief. The royal and ageing apprentice then turns, smiling, to the young master... For any observer—although no critic has observed it—

the youthfulness of Velázquez in his last self-portrait—*Las Meninas*, the great "truth"—is surprising. Velázquez was a man of almost sixty—sixty in the 17th century—without a wrinkle or a grey hair; young. And Velázquez was older than the king, the exhausted, defeated, melancholy, Philip IV, shown in his last portrait, contemporary with *Las Meninas*, in the Prado. Physiologically, Velázquez reached the peak of his powers still young; physically he had lived forty years; mentally, three centuries. Seen in this way, his work is a dazzling cataract, poured forth at incredible speed. No one has painted more in less time. Smiling, the king—prematurely old—turns towards his best friend, the eternally young Velázquez, with the watery eyes of his last years and the brush laden with blood red pigment still in his hand. Between the two there is not much difference of age; six years, more or less. But in youthful friendships which last a lifetime this small age difference can mark one type of friendship profoundly; that of the mentor, the older friend towards his younger disciple. Velázquez receives the king's tender, tearful look—insecure, timid, supplicating—with the unchanging one of the great "truth." It is difficult to imagine his eyes blurred with tears of tenderness and gratitude; tenderness and reverent and deep gratitude which are evident in his "marvellous painting." Velázquez does not weep, had not that "gift of tears" which Saint Teresa describes. In silence he takes the brush, which drips a blood red, and kisses the hand, which had solemnly given it to him twenty or more years earlier: "Tomorrow, with the proper light, I will finish your Majesty's work." And he kept his promise in a "morrow" which would last till the day of his death.

## THE STAIRCASE OF HONOUR LEADING UP TO THE GREAT "TRUTH"

The ennoblement of Velázquez with which the king celebrated the first birthday of his heir, Prince Felipe Próspero, the reign's new hope, is the last step on the staircase which, from appointment to appointment, from position to position, Velázquez had climbed in the court: king's painter in 1623, usher of the bedchamber in 1627, assistant of the wardrobe in 1636, assistant of the bedchamber in 1643, superintendent of particular works in 1648, *aposentador mayor* of the Palace in 1652... It is this brilliant court record which has given rise to the superficial classification of Velázquez as "painter and courtier." In the first place, the record is not so brilliant if one takes into account the extraordinary genius of Velázquez and his ascendancy, as older friend and mentor, over the king. "It is incredible the liberality and gratitude with which he is treated by so great a monarch," his father-in-law Francisco Pacheco declares, overwhelmed, in his book *The Art of Painting*, and he goes on to point out the reasons for his amazement: "To have a workshop in his gallery and his Majesty a key to it, and a chair to watch him slowly painting, almost every day. But what exceeds every privilege is that when he portrayed him on horseback he kept him sitting for the three hours, suspending so much energy and so much greatness."

No, his record at court is not a brilliant record for a "courtier" so sure of his incredible ascendancy over the king. But his record is not that of a "courtier" but of a "professional." Velázquez was a professional in the service of a great friend. In all his posts he acted as a technician. He was, for example, assistant of the wardrobe for seven years —and dress in the court of Philip IV, *la moda velazqueña*, as we have heard it described over and over again, was an isolated phenomenon, extraordinarily brilliant, unique, among 17th-century European fashions—. And it lasted as long as Velázquez lived. The last farthingale in 17th-century portraiture is the one which the infanta María Teresa is wearing on the day of her engagement to Louis XIV in the pavilion on the Isle of Pheasants on the river Bidasoa—not painted by Velázquez this time, but woven by the Gobelins in the famous tapestry commemorating the royal engagement, designed by Le Brun—. It is not absurd to think that Velázquez, assistant of the wardrobe, may have been the creator of the fantastic court apparel of the Spanish Austrias. The parade of his models on the historical catwalk of his royal portraits is unforgettable. In his only portrait of Queen Mariana of Austria, the impressive dress; black velvet underlined with rows of silver braid, with touches of crimson satin ribbon here and there, crimson brushstrokes scattered too over the great white ostrich feather which frames the pharaonic wig and the dark gold of the heavy brooches, chains and pendants, all manage to transform a fragile young girl, almost an adolescent, into the hieratic symbol of majesty. Then there is the extraordinary range of tones—ivory, sand, pearl, wax—, into which the strings of pearls, in his portrait of the Infanta María Teresa, seem almost to melt and which underline in red the folds of the complicated collar which surrounds the décolleté: There are the graceful arabesques on the black lace cuffs of the enchanting child's version of the farthingale in the portrait of the lady Empress doña Margarita María of Austria at a very early age, surrounded by her attendants and the muted tones of green and grey, in silk and velvet, of the dresses worn by these attendants, which, without losing their feminine appeal, are graceful versions of a lady-in-waiting's uniform... And the pink and silver skirt constructed from two panels and the black lace collar and cuffs in the first portrait of the charming Margarita... Pink and silver which would return in the sumptuous salmon coloured farthingale with diagonal silver stripes which she wears, now fully grown, a large transparent handkerchief in her hand and a soft ostrich plume, dyed red, framing her long, blonde hair... Who can forget, though it is less often seen, that other portrait of Margarita, dressed in "midnight blue" velvet, as designers would say, with its great muff of dark sables resting on the farthingale...?

To sum up: the wardrobe of the Spanish court during the Velázquez period reflects the personal taste of an artist, himself very personal. One must not forget the bold combination of pink and blue in the modest, almost feminine draperies of the crudest masculine nude in Spanish painting—the disconcerting *Mars*—, nor the combination of colours and textures in the bed on which the Venus of the Mirror is reposing; the stiff silk of dark plum colour stretched over the soft linen sheet, the black tulle or mantilla which seems to veil the hidden forehead of the female nude, the great red satin curtain in front of which there quivers a pink ribbon (shocking pink, the Schiaparelli pink of our own sixties) over the rectangular mirror's black ebony frame... The beautiful naked woman lying on her bed, slender, dark, elegant, and her stylised surroundings have nothing to do with the blonde, opulent Danäes, Venuses and Graces of Titian or Rubens, his immediate predecessors, but a great deal with the extravagant elegance of the royal wardrobe...

Palomino gives us an interesting fact to confirm the hypothesis that Velázquez, assistant of the wardrobe, was himself the designer of court fashion, where he describes his unparalleled elegance at the ceremony on the Isle of Pheasants: "In the colour of the cloth; it is no wonder he excelled, because he had better understanding of such things and always showed very good taste." Velázquez had designed his own costume and was a recognized expert on fabrics. Fashion design and knowledge of fabrics did not come from Pacheco's academy in Seville, but from his "professional" work as wardrobe assistant to the palace. If I remember rightly, Michelangelo, too, designed the uniform for the Papal Guard.

Velázquez was never a courtier in the pejorative sense of the word; he was much more, in every sense. But the red cross of Santiago on the black doublet dazzled the modest provincial intellectual who was Acisclo Antonio Palomino. His name seems to define his character: Acisclo Antonio, a name with classical and Roman resonances, followed by a modest Palomino, from Seville. His confusion was so great that he launched into a series of lucubrations, taking his pen in hand as Acisclo Antonio and dipping it profusely in the inkpot as Palomino:

> In the year 1652 His Majesty granted don Diego Velázquez the favour of *aposentador* of his imperial palace, succeeding don Pedro de Torres, in this position and he remained in it till the year 1660, when he died, exercising it to His Majesty's entire satisfaction and pleasure... This was a great honour for Velázquez; although there are some who doubt whether he needed this position of higher responsibility; because it seems that there ought to be a great difference between the rewards bestowed on gifted men and those for other kinds of merit or services; because when these come

to men who are unoccupied, the reward increases their merit by giving them an occupation: but in professional men the prize defrauds them of merit, because, if this was founded on the exercise of their gift, it will be hard for them to continue to earn it if they have no occasion to use it; and so the rewards for artists ought to be purely honorific and pecuniary (when they are precisely personal): honorific to stimulate and reward excellence; and pecuniary so that they can perfect at leisure the most hidden beauties of their art, caring only for their fame in posterity, giving then more and more opportunities to increase their honour by the perfection of their studies; this is the reward which best assures the excellence of the artist; because to hinder the use of his talent albeit with honourable duties, is a kind of reward which seems to wear the guise of punish-

> ment, because a person who has been remiss in the administration of his office is suspended from exercising it [...].

And further on, the great Palomino goes on scribbling:

> The post of *aposentador de Palacio*, besides being one of great honour, is one of so much confusion that it needs a man's full time and although we professors of painting are so proud that Velázquez has been raised to such exalted positions, we are also grieved to have lost many more testimonies of his rare ability which would have multiplied his gifts to posterity [...].

"This recitation of Velázquez' quest for wealth and position makes him appear like a brazen opportunist, who forsook a great talent to pursue the vain and ephemeral rewards of royal service," Jonathan Brown asserts shamelessly:

> But this retrospective judgement is unfair. In his time, his success at court would have been received with admiration and envy, not only by other painters but also by poets, playwrights, scholars and indeed, by virtually the entire society. Also there is no reason to believe that he lost interest or faith in the art of painting.

Evidently, there is no reason to think so; he had just finished painting the best picture in the world. It is surprising that, during three centuries, from his first biographer, Acisclo Antonio Palomino at the end of the 17th century, to the latest, Jonathan Brown at the end of the 20th, the "Velázquez case" has always focussed on the study and analysis of the incompatibility between his two activities: painting and the court. Painter and courtier—less or more painter than courtier, less or more courtier than painter...—. That seems to be the only question of interest. That is to say, to see to which side the balance tips towards the painter or the courtier. And why. Why should the great painter have begun to neglect his painting and to devote himself to designing finery or to decorating salons...? The explanation is different in the two biographies, diametrically opposed.

For Palomino, the ever scantier output of Velázquez the painter was due to the mistaken, unintelligent, way in which Philip IV, as friend and as king, rewarded his dazzling artistic career.

Palomino arrived in Madrid fifteen or twenty years after Velázquez had died. He did not know Velázquez' work except for a few youthful productions from his Seville period, and from the enthusiastic accounts of Pacheco, his father-in-law and critic. But he had caught a spark of genius on finding himself one day in front of *Las Meninas*: "It is truth, not painting." That is to say, Velázquez had transformed painting, what was generally understood as painting, into "something else" into "truth." Into what truth...? Obviously, Palomino was too close to that "atomic bomb" to measure its consequences. It embittered him to see Velázquez as a dazzling "promise," hindered—perhaps cut short—by the short-sighted attitude of the king: "Because to suspend the use of his powers"—of his genius—"with honorific duties is a reward which seems to wear the guise of punishment...." For Palomino, the blame for Velázquez having been inexplicably sidetracked into becoming a courtier lay entirely with the king. The king was the guilty party.

For Brown the ever scantier productivity of Velázquez the painter was due to the social ambitions—nobility, fortune—of Velázquez the courtier: "Years ago, José Ortega y Gasset asserted that the principal motivating force in Velázquez' life was the desire to be a nobleman. Ortega overemphasized this hypothesis in his interpretation of the artist, but the facts of Velázquez' life in the 1640s and 1650s corroborate that this was a burning ambition. And, given this fact, it is possible that Velázquez might have come to believe that his gifts as a painter were a drawback as far as his social ambitions were concerned." Brown insists:

> We know, for instance, that in 1638 his name appeared on a list of Madrid painters who were being prosecuted by an agent of the Council of Finance for payment of back taxes in the sale of their works. It was bad enough to have paintings taxed as if they were manufactured goods; but then to have been lumped together with some very second-rate artists would have been insulting to one who had consorted with Kings and cardinals. Velázquez might have become convinced that, as a painter, he had gone as far as possible along the upward path of honour and glory. Now it was time to advance his career at court by seeking higher office in the royal household,

where, through the exercise of patience, skill and good connections, a clever person could go far. Velázquez was one of those who knew how to play the game. Using the artistic patronage of the king as the foundation of his career, he gradually piled up an impressive list of offices and emoluments.

But it was not like that; he simply received the knighthood of Santiago when he had already painted *Las Meninas*. Those honorific posts, like the position of *aposentador mayor de Palacio*, Palomino considers to be "punishments in disguise." And in fact they were "disguises." Because, really, the court promotions of Velázquez are the "disguise" for a much more important achievement on his part: his absolute freedom as a painter. His original position as "the king's painter" was relegated to the shadowy threshold of the palace's grand staircase of honour. He always retained his "workshop" in the Alcázar: the king, with brotherly affection, had installed him in the "quarters"—the closed and empty rooms so difficult for anyone else to occupy—of Prince Baltasar Carlos: but had freed him from his obligations as official painter by appointing him *aposentador*: Instead of painting vaults and galleries, pictures recording the glories of the dynasty, official portraits... he was charged with obtaining them, as *aposentador mayor*, in Spain, Italy or Flanders. Velázquez, especially in his last years, painted freely what he wanted and when he wanted. And increasingly he painted less, the essential. For this reason he could be as generous to the king as the king was to him. And he gave him the only thing that was really his: his time. Meaning, of course, the time he could actually spare—which was most of the year.

Velázquez had always painted as little as possible. His tendency, towards sparseness, towards painting only the indispensable, begins, surprisingly, with his first appointment in the court as "the king's painter" in 1623, when he was twenty four. Because "our Sevillian Velázquez," as Palomino calls him with heartfelt pride, was totally different; a creative whirlwind of paintings, readings, discoveries—impossible to hold back—. Impossible to follow. Palomino gives us a lively impression of that period:

> He showed signs of a particular inclination towards painting, and though he

demonstrated talent, quickness and tractability in every subject, in this one he excelled; to the point that he sometimes used the covers of his notebooks to sketch his ideas. His vivacity awoke in his parents' hearts a very high opinion of his cleverness, which over the course of years he employed so advantageously. They let him follow his inclination, without making him carry on with other studies, because, for this one, they found he had dedication and natural ability, or the force of his destiny. They put him under the tutelage of Francisco de Herrera (who in Andalusia is called "the old Herrera") a rigid and not very pious man, but with consummate taste in Painting and the other arts.

Within a short time he left this school and followed that of Francisco Pacheco; a person of outstanding merit and great learning and understanding of painting, on which he wrote several books and composed very elegant poems, praised by all the writers of his time.

Our adolescent genius, Velázquez, preferred the learning and intelligence of Pacheco to the taste—good or bad—of old Herrera. Taste, what's more, changes over the years; intelligence and learning are permanent. The young Velázquez, like any young artist, and with the more reason for the artist he was to be—that potentially, he was—could not accept the criteria of Herrera's "consummate taste," but, could accept, Pacheco's intelligence and learning. From childhood he "thought" painting before he painted. Fundamentally he was a cerebral painter, even in his apprenticeship. In appearance, a brilliant, sweating, indomitable colt.

For this reason, Palomino says: "Pacheco's house was the gilded cage of art." Discreetly, he does not dare to call it a "stable": "Academy and school of the best minds in Seville." And so Diego Velázquez lived happily there, continually practising his drawing, "the first element of painting and main gateway to the art." This, Pacheco himself tells us with his usual simplicity and plainness and with the truthfulness of a teacher:

> With this doctrine my son-in-law, Diego Velázquez de Silva was raised. While still a boy, he had hired a little villager who served him as model in various movements and poses, now laughing, now crying, without sparing himself any difficulty. And he made many charcoal

sketches of him and reliefs in blue paper and of others too from nature, through which he acquired skill in taking portraits. He liked to paint, with great originality and notable skill, animals, birds, fish stalls and still lifes, imitating nature perfectly, with beautiful landscapes and figures, different sorts of food and drink, fruits and poor and humble furnishings, with so much mastery in drawing and colouring that they seemed real, distinguishing himself with this talent so that he had no rivals and reaped great fame and a worthy esteem of his works, among which, one should not pass over in silence the painting which is called *The Waterseller*; who is an old man, very ill clad and with a coarse and torn smock which reveals his chest and belly with its hard, rough scabs and calluses and beside him is a boy to whom he is giving a drink. And

> this has become so celebrated that it has been kept up to the present time in the palace of El Buen Retiro.

In our own, it occupies a pre-eminent place in the Wellington Museum in London, which would have surprised Palomino even more, had he known it. Because at the end of the 17th century, so close to the production of "our Sevillian Velázquez," which would have seemed only of yesterday, it was difficult for Palomino to assert, although he guessed it, that the Velázquez who arrived in Madrid, dragging his repulsive *Waterseller*, was already the foremost painter of his time.

> [...] To differentiate himself from everyone else and follow a new course, knowing that Titian, Albert, Raphael, and

> others had got windward of him and that their fame was brighter after their death, he took advantage of his original inventiveness setting out as a challenge, to paint rustic things in strange lights and colours.

One must take note of Palomino's statement that it was Titian, Albert Dürer, Raphael and others—Veronese, Tintoretto, El Greco—and not a Pacheco or an old Herrera who had "got windward of him," which implies a surprisingly sure judgement by Velázquez in the Seville of his twenty years. And Palomino dips his pen in the inkpot, and continues: "With these beginnings and the excellent portraits which he did, not contenting himself only with making them extremely lifelike but also expressing the air and movement of his subjects"—their "air" as we would say now more concisely—"he discovered the true imitation of nature, inspiring many others to follow his powerful example, which Pacheco himself refers to, as it happened to him, painting the same kind of things in imitation." Even Pacheco, his father-in-law—"person of singular merit and much learning and understanding of painting, on which he wrote several books"—let himself be carried away by the "imaginative inventiveness" of his nineteen year old son-in-law! The colt was impetuous. "Velázquez competes with Caravaggio in the boldness of his painting and was equal to Pacheco in speculation." Note speculative—thoughtful, cerebral—. Even in the eyes of his own contemporaries Velázquez was this from the age of twenty.

Some paintings were brought to Seville from Italy which gave Velázquez a great desire to attempt enterprises no less great with his talent. They were works by the artists who flourished at that time: one Pomerancio, Caballero Baglioni, Lanfranco, Ribera, Guido and others. Those which found the most favour in his eyes were those of Luis Tristán, a painter from Toledo (disciple of Dominico Greco), because they followed a similar course to his own disposition in their singularity of ideas and their liveliness of conception; and for this reason he declared himself his imitator and ceased painting in the manner of his master, having realised, from the very beginning that such a tame way of painting did not suit him, full of learning and exact drawing though it was, being contrary to his own lofty nature and love of grandeur. He was given the name of second Caravaggio because

> he copied the natural world so happily and with so much mastery, keeping it before him in everything he did and all the time. In his portraits he imitated Dominico Greco because his heads could never be too highly praised.

The influence of El Greco on Velázquez was a Spanish dogma during the first third of our century. The dogma must have been sustained by what was termed the "cold gamut" of El Greco and Velázquez, the silvery "vistas" of Toledo and the blue landscapes of the Guadarrama—backgrounds to the equestrian and hunting portraits—as against the golden "warm gamut" of the Venetians, and by the enthusiasm of "our own" Velázquez for the works of "the painter of Toledo" glimpsed through Tristán, perhaps seen in some collection in

Seville: an enthusiasm so emphatically remarked by Palomino. But in this last third of our century, this Spanish dogma has gone with the wind. "My creed as an historian," writes Brown, "makes me sceptical of interpretations which rely more on speculation than investigation," as if information without speculation—and with closed eyes—were of any use. And where could Velázquez have seen a Greco in Seville between 1599 when he was born and 1623 when he left Seville permanently? As the most exhaustive research has produced neither a name nor an address, Palomino's speculations are valueless. End of story. Brown's attitude is unfortunately the one generally accepted today by historians. Those of us who are not historians, but observers, readers and from time to time, narrators, on happening to find in the final pages of the more than three hundred of his *Velázquez, Painter and Courtier*, fruit of the most thorough investigation, the fact that in the inventory of Velázquez' possessions, carried out by his executors three days after his death, there appear, in his workshop in the prince's quarters, "three portraits by El Greco" arrive at the conclusion that Palomino was right: El Greco influenced Velázquez throughout his life. And Velázquez' life is his work. But the historian, as he should not—and in some cases cannot—speculate, downloads the fact onto the memory of his computer and the subject is closed—Amen...

The great Palomino has again dipped his pen in the inkpot, contemplates the blank sheet of paper on the desk before him, snorts vigorously and...

"This which you see here, O pilgrim / Of shining porphyry the hard key, / Denies to the softer world the brush / Which gave spirit to canvas, life to linen." Thus begins Góngora's sonnet "At the tomb of Doménico Theotocopuli" (I quote from memory because I believe that what remains in one's mind from one's school years in the Institución Libre de Enseñanza is more important than the information photocopied in the library half an hour ago). Velázquez painted Góngora's portrait during his first visit to Madrid, in 1622, with the laurel crown of a pagan god —the laurel crown which Apollo wears when he visits Vulcan—and which he later erased so as to leave the man, Góngora, bald as he really was... Would these two refined Andalusians have talked about El Greco? What critical judgements would the great Cordovan have made on El Greco and on Velázquez, the young man who had just entered in his sombre study, as dazzling as Apollo in Vulcan's forge, with no other crown but his splendid black hair?

What did our Sevillian think of Dominico Greco? Because what he thought about Góngora X-rays have revealed to us; he rubbed out the laurels, rhetorical symbol of glory, and left bare the head of the marvellous man he saw before him. And Acisclo Palomino writes:

> He exercised himself in the reading of various authors, who have left us valuable precepts on painting: he would study

the symmetry of the human body in Albert Dürer, anatomy in Andreas Vesalius, perspective in Daniel Barbaro, physiogmony in Juan Bautista Porta, geometry in Euclid, arithmetic in Moya, architecture in Vitrubio and in Viñola, and other authors; among whom, with the diligence of a bee, he would select out for his use, and for the benefit of posterity, what was most fitting and perfect... he embellished his paintings according to the precepts of Juan Bautista and Armenini. And he learned from Michaelangelo Biondo to execute them promptly and swiftly. Vasari inspired him with his *Lives of Famous Painters* and the *Riposo* of Rafael Borghini established him as an erudite painter. He graced himself too with a knowledge of sacred and profane literature and other important things to enrich his mind with every branch of learning and a universal understanding of the arts.

The young Apollo was a thinking painter, a modern intellectual, a free spirit in search of himself, of his own "truth."

## THE GREAT "TRUTH" IS EVERYWHERE

On the 30th of August, 1623, Velázquez paints the first portrait of Philip IV. Having returned to Seville with the portrait of Góngora in his luggage, he came back to Madrid, recalled by Pacheco's Seville friends, a few months later, in the first days of August. Thanks to a rapid and well-executed intrigue by the Seville party, the king had consented to be painted by Velázquez. The visit of the Prince of Wales, at the same time, delayed the execution of the royal order until the 30th. But on the morning of that day "our Velázquez" set up his easel in one of the galleries of the Palace, perhaps the one later to be that "of the Prince's quarters" where *Las Meninas* were painted.

And the king entered. He was a youth of eighteen, slender, tall, fair, dressed all in black and wearing hat and gloves; "gloves of amber," in grey suede and a black hat with a high, almost cylindrical crown and a straight, narrow brim. No one may shake or kiss the bare hand of this pharaonic monarch, nor does the king have to doff his hat to anyone. Velázquez reverently kissed the king's gloved hand, scented with ambergris, and the king greeted him with the timid smile of someone receiving a gift he does not think he deserves. The king looked very young, with a pink, childlike complexion, almost transparent, through which his blue-blooded veins could be seen; the shy look of an intelligent child; very full, red lips, terribly sensual. The black of his sober costume was relieved only by a heavy gold chain crossing his chest diagonally and the sparkle of a little Golden Fleece hanging from a soft black silk ribbon, which, when he moved, tinkled against the links of the chain at the height of his slender waist, emphasising the supreme elegance of this almost adolescent youth. The king took off his gloves and laid his hat on a desk covered in red velvet with gold cords at the corners and placed himself silently on the model's bench facing the painter's easel... The few courtiers, the multi-coloured dwarf, and the great dog which had come in with him, moved discreetly to one side... It would be wonderful to be able to tell, with the successive shots of a "candid camera," the precise moment when the two young men felt the current of affection pass between them which was to unite them and make them fast friends for life: Perhaps it was when the king, in an unguarded moment, bent forward to see how the picture was getting on and pushed the "tablet of colours," making it fall noisily to the ground with the immediate movement of a younger brother who is going to stoop to pick it up, something which his elder instantly prevented, with a brilliant smile: Perhaps... But at some time the picture was painted and, a few weeks later, Velázquez received his appointment as the king's painter. With the promise, according to Pacheco, that he was the only painter who would portray him from that time forth.

Velázquez must have been deeply impressed by the restrained elegance and austere grandeur of the House of Austria. The exquisite taste of the court, solemn and simple, popular and erudite, personified by the king, and the barely glimpsed style of El Greco, were to be the two great influences in the new phase of this second Caravaggio, aged twenty-four, of this Apollo in Vulcan's forge, this destroyer of the traditional symbols of glory. Because glory is a moral value which cannot be seen. And isn't it the same with art? Góngora, in print, looks like any other book; one needs to read him. Doesn't painting, in one way or another, need to be read?

Velázquez was appointed as the king's painter on the 6th of October, 1623, a few weeks after his visit to the king. The colt was now a man. With one clean stroke, he severed himself from his brief immediate past. Goodbye, second Caravaggio! Goodbye little village model laughing and crying, waterseller with his coarse and torn smock, poor men eating at a simple table. Goodbye, clay cups, oranges, bread... Goodbye to the dogs eying sea bream and other fish like sardines, to long romaine lettuces, loaves of Seville bread on a white cloth, white clay plates, little clay oil jug with a greenish glaze. ("And he put his name on this painting although it is now very worn and blurred by time," says Palomino.) Goodbye, tinker's furnace, little tin kettle, porous water jar, plates and bowls, glazed pitcher, brass mortar with its pestle... Goodbye, bulb of garlic cloves! He had painted the king; never, as long as he lived, would he paint another still life.

But he painted very little in these first years as the king's painter. In fact, he adopted what was to be the norm throughout his life: to paint the essential. He must have spent his time, which passed much more quickly than the hands of the sumptuous Palace clocks in mahogany, bronze and silver, hours weeks, months, years... in going through the galleries of the Palace, studying, thinking about the already outstanding royal collection of paintings, during long periods in El Escorial; its collections, the imposing structure of the building, "eighth wonder of the world." And how many hours must he not have spent in Toledo, in the church of Santo Tomé, in front of *The Burial of the Count of Orgaz?*

A bright orange rolling across a floor of worn, old tiles suddenly comes to my mind when I remember Santo Tomé in the twilight of the dying day and the harsh glare of the electric lights which are being switched on—and the superb *Burial* shines here, there, from whichever spot one looks at it. It was the first time that, as a boy, with my great friend since childhood, Antonio Jiménez-Landi, I found myself alone, without teachers and companions from the "Insti," facing the great picture, when an orange fell out of my raincoat pocket and rolled across the floor.

The "Insti" is what we, little larval Institutionists, used to call the Institución Libre de Enseñanza, as pupils of that remarkable foundation, already then somewhat in decline, from primary school up to the final years of the Baccalaureate. Its founder, don Francisco Giner de los Ríos, had already died and Picasso's scandalous *Demoiselles d'Avignon* had been on show for years. The death of don Francisco was recalled in the verses of Antonio Machado, who sometimes came to collect his nieces, the daughters of his brother, the painter Pepe Machado:

"When the master left us, the morning light told me: for some days now brother Francisco has not been working," which were recited punctually on every anniversary: Picasso and his *Demoiselles* were ignored. The headmaster —or rather the living spirit of the Institución—was señor Cossío, Manuel Bartolomé Cossío, teacher and art critic, the Spanish discoverer of El Greco. The Institución had closed its doors to modern art with Sorolla... But, even in the youngest classes, we went on one afternoon a week to the Prado Museum and on another to play football in Chamartín, then on the outskirts of Madrid; a football field among olive trees, very near the houses where Ramón Menéndez Pidal and José Castillejo lived. On some Sundays we went on excursions to El Escorial, to Toledo, to Alcalá de Henares... and when we were older, boys and girls, co-education was one of the pillars of *institucionista* education, we spent an occasional weekend without our parents—but with teachers, of course—free on our own, in a modest hotel in Avila, Salamanca or Zamora. The Institución ignored social classes; I shared a desk with the porter's daughter from the house opposite mine. The seniors sometimes made week long trips to Seville, Cordova, Granada. And now and then, they spent a weekend skiing in the Guadarrama mountains... Because the Institución, which made the smallest, larval *institucionista* learn by heart *El Cantar del Mio Cid* in its original 11th-century text, had promoted in the Spain of bullfights and fives courts, two recently introduced foreign sports: football and skiing. We did have, nonetheless, a fives court in the old garden of the "Insti" and, unconfessable shame, which I never had to confess —I had been to a bullfight one Sunday afternoon! In the Salon of the Institución, tea was served at five o'clock, in the English fashion. In spite of the tea, all the most outstanding personalities of Spain at that time—the turn of the century—have passed through the Salon of the Institución.

In this Europeanising atmosphere —philosophically the Institución had been modelled on German "Krausism"—socially on English customs, our "Insti" had promoted authentic folk art, which, logically, excluded Manila shawls and—God knows why!—castanets... (Falla did not pass through the Institución but, years later, Lorca did, though tangentially.)

An amiable sacristan, with the long candle snuffer of his calling, rescued my orange from under the bench where it had hidden itself and put it in my hand.

And he explained to me his personal theory on the ideal lighting for the *Burial*, the fruit of long years of observation and experiment; the electric light, introduced early in the century to "modernise" the church, makes the old picture shine, from wherever you approach it and wherever you look; the picture was not painted to be lit by electric reflectors, so much is obvious; but if, at night, with the church in darkness, three lighted torches are placed just in front of and at the same distance from the three lighted torches in the picture —the picture will not shine! How Velázquez would have appreciated this sacristan of Santo Tomé, untaught but erudite in his limited field, he who had studied the lighting of the royal collections in the galleries of El Alcázar and

El Escorial! Very probably with the same technical result: Light should reach the picture as it is shown to come in the picture itself. But, in most of the great pictures which he was hanging, the light does not arrive from any particular direction. A uniform, diffuse, even light is what they receive in the long galleries where, framed by columns and stucco, hung against velvet-covered walls, they are transformed into flat expanses—magic, surprising displays of design and colour—enclosed in their rectangular gilt frames; they are converted into decorations for architectural spaces. Like the Roman frescoes or the Byzantine mosaics. Like the tapestries. The portraits are simply "identity cards." And Velázquez, the king's painter, decides to paint the indispensable, and to go on painting in his mind, imagining subjects, compositions, colour, light, shadows, in his long hours of study in the Palace galleries, in El Escorial, in Toledo; sitting, alone and pensive in his studio; revising plans for the reform of the Alcázar... or reading in a corner of his room. Because the great "truth," guessed at since Seville, is to be found everywhere.

## THE DOOR OF THE GREAT "TRUTH" STARTS TO OPEN

In September 1628, Rubens arrives in Madrid.

The analysis, in part by X-rays, of the historic meeting between the great Peter Paul Rubens, one of the consecrated masters of pictorial art, a *monstre sacré*, as we would say today, and the young king's painter, who was already usher of the bedchamber—think of that!—is fundamental to an understanding of Velázquez. Fortunately, all the contemporary documents marking the historic occasion have been preserved; almost everything that Rubens painted in Madrid and everything which Velázquez painted during his long visit, which naturally was not much; the sacred monster, burdened with years, painted much more than he did. A consecrated man is one who has passed into history. When the unknown Velázquez "gave him his arms" which is how the greeting was described in those days—he must have felt he was embracing, in flesh and blood, a glorious past—as though, returning one afternoon from the Prado, he were to have met Titian... But first, let us read the accounts which Velázquez' first and latest biographers, Palomino and Jonathan Brown, give of this meeting. The first says:

> [...] Peter Paul Rubens came to Spain (prodigy of talent, of ability and of fortune) as different authors tell and is published in his works, as Ambassador Extraordinary from the king of England to arrange the peace with Spain,

through the wish of the Archduke Albert and his wife, Her Serene Highness doña Isabel Clara Eugenia, through their high opinion of Rubens and the great fame of his learning and talent.

With painters (as Pacheco says) he consorted little; only with Velázquez (with whom he had communicated before by letter) did he become a very close friend and favoured his work because of his great merit and modesty; and they went together to El Escorial, to see the celebrated monastery of San Lorenzo; they both took special delight in seeing and admiring the many marvellous prodigies in that sublime edifice; and especially the original paintings of the greatest artists who have flourished in Europe; whose example gave Velázquez a new stimulus to inflame the desire he had always had to travel to Italy to see, speculate on and study those eminent

> works and statues which are the resplendent torches of art and worthy subjects of admiration.

The general tone of Palomino's brief report reflects the cordiality of the meeting between the two great artists—no frequent thing, either then or now—besides which, so different; the glorious monster facing the "modest" monster Palomino's adjective is just. Cordiality of the greater to the lesser, which is natural, almost instinctive among dogs, is not always so, among men... Palomino mentions a correspondence previous to the meeting between Rubens and Velázquez where one can trace the diplomatic hand of the Infanta Isabel Clara Eugenia, the king's aunt and governor of the Low Countries; having learned of the king's friendship with the painter —courts are gilded villages where everything is known and commented on—she suggested a first contact with Velázquez, from painter to painter, as this was the most direct route of entry to the king's inner circle. At all events, Rubens and Velázquez struck up "a very close friendship." But in what language did they understand each other...? Probably from easel to easel, seeing each other paint. Rubens painted during the months he spent in Madrid, a bust of the king, a full length portrait of the king, an enormous equestrian portrait of the king and he copied, revitalising them, Titian's *Adam and Eve* and the *Rape of Europa*. Velázquez only managed to paint one picture, *The Triumph of Bacchus* or *The Topers*. Communication from easel to easel is a kind of fax, much more rapid than the electronic one, and much more compromising. As compromising as a psychoanalysis. Especially in the hands of two communicators as sensitive as Rubens and Velázquez. Rubens must have been scandalised by the perilous daring, the destructive force, the, to him, almost pathological motivation of Velázquez and his incomprehensible pictorial message; in what language was he speaking? No, the influence of this seductive Sevillian was a danger for any transaction. "He favoured his works" and convinced the king—the painter was already more than convinced—that he should send the young genius to Italy as soon as possible, for a long stay. Velázquez, who was no courtier and had only marginal interest in the peace with England, seized the occasion by the hair and, two months after Rubens had left Madrid, the unsettling usher of the bedchamber embarked for the first time in Barcelona "to pass into Italy, to see, speculate and study." In those two months he repainted his first portrait of the king and framed *The Topers*, symbol of his revolt, unexpected and violent, like the sudden dash of an Andalusian colt, against the golden magnificence of Rubens.

The "analysis"—as the press would say nowadays—of Brown's account of Rubens' visit to Madrid coincides basically, as regards the facts, with Palomino's, but, as always, differs totally in its conclusions. One has to gather his point of view from his extensive account of

Rubens' visit, "the third visit by an artist in those years... undoubtedly the most important." But there is one really important fact which Palomino does not mention and Brown tells us:

> Knowing in advance of the king's love of pictures, the artist had brought eight of his works, an assortment of biblical and mythological subjects and hunting scenes. In addition, his appearance in Madrid coincided with the arrival of one of his masterpieces, the magnificent series of tapestries for the royal convent of the Descalzas Reales. Rubens' art, which had been represented in Madrid by a few examples only, now became a force to reckon with.

"During his stay at court, Rubens added to this stock of pictures in ways which were instructive to the king and his painter," Brown continues analysing: "First he executed a group of royal portraits, thus infringing on Velázquez' monopoly." It seems that he painted first "a bust-length" portrait of the king. "More impressive is the full-length image of the king. Here it seems as if Rubens made use of a composition by Velázquez" (the first and only portrait of the king which existed at that time, painted by Velázquez). "It is tempting to think that Rubens intended these portraits as a lesson to the young artist, but this may be imagining too much." We respect the fear of imagining, the refusal to speculate, to think, which his "faith as a historian" enjoins on this conscientious scholar; that is up to him. But we will accept the lesson implicit in Rubens' portrait of the king and analyse radiographically how Velázquez received the lesson. We will follow Brown: "Velázquez painted a full-length portrait which some years later, he extensively repainted." The repainted version is the portrait of Philip IV, which remains in the Prado. "Fortunately the original composition was twice recopied before it was reworked," copies, which are now in the Metropolitan Museum in New York and the Boston Museum of Fine Arts, "...and with the help of these pictures and a radiograph of the reworked portrait" —the one in the Prado—"it is easily reconstructed." It is the immediate predecessor of the twin portrait of the infante don Carlos, also in the Prado, but more solemn, less freely elegant. The king is dressed like the prince, from head to foot in black, with the same heavy gold chain across his chest—it seems that this was the latest court fashion—and a little Golden Fleece hanging from a soft, black ribbon. But in his right hand he holds a folded sheet of paper and the prince a glove, dangling with careless elegance from a fingertip, and he holds his big, black hat in his gloved left hand; the king wears no gloves and his hat is on a desk covered in red velvet with gold cords at the corners. Rubens evidently used this first version of the king's portrait as a basis for his own portrait, "deftly transforming it" according to Brown, "into a model of sophisticated, up-to-date court portraiture"—up to date then—, he means, of course.

> Posing his sitter in a logia-like setting with a distant landscape, Rubens creates an air

of magnificence through the use of a giant column cloaked with luxuriant drapery, which imparts a singing motion to the composition. Next to this confident demonstration of pictorial mastery, Velázquez' portrait lacks space, drama and finesse.

All this leads one to think that Velázquez, after seeing Rubens' "sophisticated and up-to-date" portrait, immediately decided to transform his own. The "lesson" did have an immediate effect, though a totally unexpected one. Perhaps Velázquez, the elegant courtier—the court imposed a code of social manners—waited till Rubens had left to repaint his portrait; he eliminated the great gold chain "in the latest fashion" to make the king more personally distinguished, he eliminated the desk's gold cords, obviously palatial, to emphasize his royal majesty unadorned, against a vague background of greys and dark crimsons, and he stylised, a little like El Greco, the king's slender figure, by changing the somewhat defiant position of his left leg—the careless attitude of the infante don Carlos—almost joining his two feet. This is how the portrait of Philip IV has remained for history "lacking space, drama and finesse," an image which, since the generation of '98 "translated" into literature by Manuel Machado: "All in black unto his feet attired" has personified the highest moment of Spanish culture, the Golden Age, the final splendour of the Spanish empire...

Brown goes on to inform us:

> In the last months of 1628, Rubens created a monumental equestrian portrait of

the king, now known only in a later copy... Upon completion, this portrait was installed in the new gallery of the Alcázar, taking the place of the *Philip IV on Horseback* executed by Velázquez and triumphantly shown in public just three years before.

Court etiquette prevailed: The Velázquez was taken down and the Rubens enthroned, but not for long. Rubens' royal portraits cannot have formed a permanent part of the royal collection, as none of them have arrived at the Prado and the originals, or their copies where the originals have been lost, are all to be found outside Spain. But the different means used by Rubens to "instruct" the king and his painter had some effect. The commissions to Rubens continued, despite the mediocre royal portraits painted in Madrid, so rhetorical, flatulent and vacuous that they do not seem to be Rubens. Did Velázquez and the pharaonic atmosphere of the court have a negative influence on the great master of Baroque? Upon his death, the king, undoubtedly advised by Velázquez, did everything possible to obtain, in the auction of his works, the best pictures from Rubens' personal collection. And he succeeded, with the superb collection of Rubens, now in the Prado. In the same way as the Japanese today buy Van Goghs, to enjoy the unfading beauty of a world which has irrevocably ended.

Brown goes on to write:

> Pacheco mentions that Rubens ignored the other court painters and kept only

the company of Velázquez. The two went together to El Escorial to look at pictures and undoubtedly talked at length about what they saw. There is, of course, no written record of this and other encounters, but there is a painted one, which survives in the remarkable series of copies after Titian done by Rubens. These copies are usually understood as an act of homage by a great master to a revered and kindred spirit of the past. But they can also be understood as a kind of lesson from a brilliant, experienced painter to a brilliant, inexperienced painter.

It is interesting to note that—finally!—Brown accepts speculation as a way to understand "painted testimonies," but what follows shows that speculation is not the historian's strong point: "Velázquez knew the paintings of Titian by heart, but had not been able to penetrate the reach of their greatness. Rubens, however, had seen and understood." And further on: "When we place Velázquez' first major mythological painting, *The Triumph of Bacchus*, which was done while Rubens was still at court, alongside Rubens' copy of *The Rape of Europa* we see how much Velázquez still had to learn to meet the standards of a great Baroque artist." That this should be said in the 20th century is really scandalous, because Velázquez never aspired to be a Baroque painter, but quite the contrary. But neither did he have anything more to learn —rather, he had learned too much—to be one. To our eyes today *The Topers* pierce through the wall of the museum, opening a great door onto a scene which is fantastic and familiar—alive and luminous—one smells and hears it. Beside it, today, Rubens' copy of Titian's *Rape of Europa* is hardly visible. This is an experience which anyone can have, spending fifteen minutes in the Prado Museum where "Velázquez' first major mythological painting" is placed very close to the Rubens copy.

For the sensibility and critical judgement—information added to speculation—of a viewer today, the Velázquez who Rubens knew in Madrid is much more interesting than the Rubens Velázquez knew. The same applies to his works, although we are considering only what he had produced up to that time (between September, 1628, and May, 1629). *The Triumph of Bacchus*, painted with the rebelliousness of an Andalusian colt who will not be mounted, smashes against his canvas the whole concept of "decorative" painting, if we can use the word "decorative," which has now a pejorative sense when applied to painting, in its original meaning of "ornamental," of beautifying a bare space; like a tapestry which covers a wall. Something, which Velázquez had much in mind, having just seen Rubens' series of tapestries for the Descalzas Reales, where they still remain. This theme of decorative painting, of the picture as "tapestry cartoon," preoccupies Velázquez throughout his life; it is revealing that the tapestry showing Arachne, which is the background to his picture *The Weavers*, should be the "tapestry version" of Titian's *Rape of Europa* copied by Rubens in Madrid thirty years before. No; a picture should not decorate a wall, like a tapestry; it should break through it, open a hole into another world, the world of imagination, of thought. Although it seems paradoxical, the most realistic of painters is always the most cerebral. And here it is, in the "hole" made by *The Topers*, the imagined world, the world thought by Velázquez; rebellion, creation... He swept away all the principles of composition, piling up the old topers in a corner at one side, like a heap of wineskins; leaving empty the other side where a kneeling youth is waiting to be crowned deacon of the new rite... Bacchus, a half naked boy crowned with vine leaves, almost an adolescent "whose beard has not begun to sprout" stops for a moment to listen to what the man, apparently quite naked, who is lying by his side, is saying to him. The naked man, already crowned with vine tendrils, holds a goblet of wine in his left hand; with his right, he clutches a corner of Bacchus' robe, as if to seize it and leave him altogether naked... The picture smells of wine; white, transparent wine like the generous wines of Andalusia; so transparent that through it one can see the sky in the background, the sky of the Pardo... One hears a murmur, the murmur of the breeze in the nearby oak grove, the whispered council which the naked man is giving to the boy? The picture is enigmatic; one needs to "listen" to it once more, to read it, like Góngora, again and again... Many years after the picture was painted, Palomino enumerates the statues which Velázquez brought back from Italy on his second journey, and describes: "Also a Bacchus, a boy leaning against a tree-trunk on which his clothes are hanging, his right arm is raised and in his hand a bunch of grapes." Could this youthful Bacchus, who strips to celebrate the triumph of wine, which Velázquez perceived intuitively before he went to Italy, be his brilliant contribution to the "collections of emblems" so frequently consulted in 17th-century Spain?

## THE GREAT "TRUTH" IS NOT IN ROME

All roads lead to Rome. That is to say: they led to Rome in the 17th century. But the great "truth" was not in Rome...

Velázquez returned from his first Italian journey—centred on Rome—with two great and profoundly disconcerting pictures: *Vulcan's Forge* and *Joseph's Brothers*. Disconcerting because the man who had just painted his first mythological picture, *The Triumph of Bacchus*, does not seem the same as the one who afterwards, in the same line of production—we will put Joseph's biblical brothers in the same bottomless sack of mythology—was to paint those brothers with the bloody remnant of Joseph's tunic, torn to shreds, against a background of renaissance columns unimaginable in a biblical setting; and the rosy Apollo crowned with laurels —a crown which he had removed from Góngora's brow some years earlier—in a forge too dusty for the *Odyssey*, too spacious for the *Iliad*, where Vulcan, a smith from Trastevere, is surrounded by professional models from the academy of fine art... What has become of the heap of drunken wineskins; the youth crowned with vine leaves, timid and foolish, who does not dare to shed his clothes; of the murmur, the scent and the freshness of the Pardo; of the transparent goblet of Andalusian wine, indeed of that door opening onto the truth on the other side of the wall, the great truth of the world of imagination? The two great pictures—great in every way, naturally—must have caused the surprise one feels uncovering a "transfer," still damp, after anxious expectation—the long stay in Italy.

First the king and, after him, the whole court, must have gathered, as in *Las*

*Meninas*, to look at the great canvases newly arrived from Italy, hanging in the workshop of the king's painter, now resplendent usher of the bedchamber. This great dazzling surprise, Velázquez' two "Italian" pictures, must have resounded like a knock on the door of the Alcázar; Velázquez had arrived, converted into a great master of painting. Because his two pictures really are "painting," as Palomino would say; not so much "truth." The king must have had a great surprise, seeing the gap in the wall, recently opened by *The Triumph of Bacchus*, closed again. But it is very possible that the most surprised of all, at finding himself back in Madrid facing his two "Italian" canvases, may have been Velázquez: Had he wasted his journey and his time? (Not all roads lead to Rome...)

The trajectory, the professional evolution of Velázquez, from Pacheco's academy until his return from Rome at the beginning of 1631, is the trajectory of any great painter, but seen through a magnifying glass, a magic lens, the product of several centuries of elaboration. This magnifying lens was not in our hands until the beginning of this century. Picasso himself has put it on the table of any inquiring person. Palomino, of course, could not use it—but Ortega and Brown could, and did not even see it—. What is more, they did not want to see it and discreetly elbowed it aside.

Yes, the evolution of Velázquez is the evolution of any great painter—Picasso, for example—, but magnified through the wonderful crystal of time, the lens of four centuries: Both children were precocious; Velázquez filled the covers of his school folders with drawings of little villagers, laughing and crying. Picasso painted the tiny feet of the pigeons in his father's pictures, the intelligent art teacher, señor Ruiz, whose eyesight no longer enabled him to copy from nature the fragile feet of his pigeon models, with a mastery which astonished the art teacher himself... Both fathers decided to send their sons to art school—señor Ruiz partly through inertia but, much more, in the hope that his son would achieve what he had not succeeded in—and señor de Silva, Velázquez' father, despite the fact that, in the 17th century, painting was not a gentlemanly profession and though not a gentleman himself, he was vain like all

Portuguese, especially outside their own country. Both realised that their sons were artists of genius and—with financial sacrifices in the case of señor Ruiz, and the sacrifice of aristocratic pretensions in that of señor de Silva—they did the same thing.

Picasso himself, during a long afternoon, which I spent with other friends in his house in Valloris, told me in great detail about his first experiences as a professional painter of pigeon's feet. "As we were very poor," he said, "the model pigeon which my father had painted during the day, except for the feet, we ate for supper." Afterwards they pinned the little feet with great care in the required position on a cork base. And those little pink feet, dextrously maintained in the proper pose, were painted by the infant Pablo Ruiz Picasso with the same dexterity with which they had been positioned. "All through my life," Picasso said, looking at me with his big wide eyes—the same eyes which had looked intensely at his delicate models, eighty years before—"I have painted, I have drawn, I have engraved, thousands of pigeons, some of them reproduced in their turn, on thousands of posters distributed all over the world... Each one of those pigeons is a remembrance, a tribute to my father who supported me with so much effort to enable me to do it." Could the aristocratic atmosphere in which Velázquez produced all his masterpieces have been a way of rewarding the aristocratic ambition of his father, who bowed his head and put him in a school of "artisans"? A tribute to

Diego de Silva from his son, don Diego de Silva, Knight of Santiago?

The two youthful geniuses—Velázquez and Picasso—quickly and triumphantly exhausted the possibilities offered by their respective academies; the "old" Herrera and Pacheco and the school of San Fernando. And they set out to make their way in their respective art worlds; Velázquez in Seville, a new Caravaggio, since "Titian, Albert Dürer, Raphael, and others," no less, had "got windward of him"; Picasso in Barcelona, triumphing over Casas, admired by intellectuals and the upper classes. Everyone knows the story of Picasso's youthful exploits and his great exhibition of portraits "after Casas" in the café Els Quatre Gats. At age twenty, Velázquez and Picasso had risen to the top of their respective artistic milieux, Seville at the start of the 17th century, and the Barcelona of the 1890s. Success pushed them much higher; Velázquez, the king's painter at twenty-four; Picasso, in Paris at about the same age, paints and exhibits *Les Demoiselles d'Avignon*, the most important picture of the 20th century, according to Alfred H. Barr, founder and first director of the Museum of Modern Art in New York.

But we are here with the king and his painter, as surprised as they are, confronting the two great "Italian" pictures… Because if we apply the magnifying lens, that magic glass of time, to the last picture Velázquez painted before he left for Italy, *The Triumph of Bacchus*, we see that *The Topers* are obviously closer to Manet's *Dejeuner sur l'Herbe* than to Titian's *Bacchanal.* Which implies that, chronologically, *Vulcan's Forge* and *Joseph's Brothers* represent a retrogression in Velázquez' work of over two centuries!

But the two friends, the king and Velázquez, had so much to discuss and confide to each other that they closed the painter's workshop to shut themselves up during the long, most private hours of the night, in the office of the king's quarters. What is clear is that the style of Velázquez' first Italian journey passed rapidly into history; *Joseph's Brothers* went to El Escorial; who knows where *Vulcan's Forge* ended up? And Velázquez' subsequent production shows the perpetual zigzagging of the king's painter to carry out his official duties. (Of course, the king's painter was now usher of the bedchamber which in many cases, implied the priority of this function... Which is to say, he could choose who would paint this or that when he, Velázquez, was not interested in doing it.)

## ZIGZAGGING TOWARDS THE GREAT "TRUTH"

The changing direction, the continual zigzagging in Velázquez' productions between his two Italian journeys (from 1628 till 1648, twenty key years) is a labyrinth which is very difficult to enter and from which it is almost impossible to get out. One would need to find Arachne's ball of thread, which Velázquez held in his hand, whose end, curiously takes us beyond the labyrinth and Velázquez' return from his second Italian journey to his last mythological picture, *The Fable of Arachne* or *The Weavers.*

What seems evident is that the entrance to the labyrinth is to be found in the office of the king's quarters "in those most exclusive hours when the gentlemen and courtiers have retired," when the two friends, the king and Velázquez, are left alone together, face to face. The pictures which initiate this zigzagging period make one think that Velázquez entered the labyrinth, not in search of the great "truth," but pushed, through affection, to follow his younger friend, his Catholic Majesty, King Philip. The king had lost his youthful timidity; the Kingdom seemed to have shaken off the lethargy of Philip III's reign; the count-duke had already mounted the triumphant horse on which Velázquez would portray him... The friend and mentor decided that he must follow—and oversee—the steps of his junior; and he painted *The Coronation of the Virgin* for the queen's oratory, which takes us back to the *Adoration of the Magi* from his Seville period. Because Velázquez seems to feel that he has gone back ten years, to the time when he first entered his workshop in the Alcázar. But at the same time like the prodigal son who returns home. And, in gratitude, he then paints, on the king's orders, his *Christ on the Cross*, with the feet nailed and apart, as the learned Pacheco advises, to respect historical truth. Seville is present again, as if Velázquez had returned from there and not from Rome.

Velázquez, in 17th-century Spain, is an outstandingly profane painter. His religious pictures can be counted on the fingers of one hand or at the most, of two hands. Compared with Zurbarán, with Ribera, with Murillo...! But, furthermore, is the *Christ on the Cross* which he has just painted, really a religious picture? It is true that it was painted to inspire greater devotion, for us to pray at its feet, which are separated, nailed to the wood with a nail in each foot, because that was how it was; to be looked at kneeling, with one's face against the icy bars of the chapel screen; to be lit only by some weak candles under the freezing darkness of the vault, like an apparition still palpitating... But the beautiful naked man who hides his face behind his long Nazarene hair evokes horror at the crime, the murder, rather than admiration for the sacrifice and the imminent glory of the resurrection. The black background, laurel green, which is almost black, after a recent cleaning (but does absolute black exist?) is the background of a cave, bounded by the rectangular frame, almost the background of a cupboard, rather than the shadowy spaces of Golgotha, against which the naked body stands out, waxen, luminous, clean. "For a bad Christ lots of blood," Velázquez' contemporaries would say jokingly, treating the subject with the same aesthetic feeling as the Italians their Saint Sebastians.

A little further into the zigzagging labyrinth through which Velázquez is travelling, there appears another masculine nude, the disconcerting *Mars.* The god Mars or the clown Mars, a madman who believed himself to be a god and Greek and went around naked, armed with a gleaming helmet and shield? (There is a madman like this, a mad god Neptune, in the prologue by Cervantes—well versed in contemporary madmen—to the second part of *Don Quixote.*) In any case, Velázquez' *Mars* is not an idealised, academic nude, but the first real "nude," perhaps the portrait of an unknown man who agreed to pose naked for the painter (a first Painter and his Model, almost a first *Minotaur?*) But what is evident in this broken succession of nudes—from

*Christ* to *Mars*—is an interest in the nude itself, detached from all religious, literary or historical connections, the nude as pictorial theme. An interest which seems to lead Velázquez to his first female nude without any justification; the admirable *Venus of the Mirror*. Because it is clear that the Baroque cupid, who holds the mirror and allows the picture its title, is a mere device to enable such a picture, the back view of a naked woman lying on her bed and looking at herself in the mirror, to hang in a 17th-century Spanish drawing room. In this sense the so-called *Venus of the Mirror* is the first "nude" in the history of painting. And continues to be so in every sense, three centuries later.

I have heard a distinguished Colombian painter make a reservation: "Yes, it may be the most beautiful nude which has ever been painted, in spite of that right arm." Because the right arm is partially hidden, visually distorted, by the pillows of the bed, covered by the great coverlet of dark, rustling silk of an almost black plum colour. The luminous body of the *Christ*, too, shines against a laurel green, almost black background, as unsuitable for a sky as the dark silk is for a bed—the bed on which the model raises herself to look in the mirror...—and at that moment is surprised by the painter in all her dazzling beauty. That right arm, half hidden in the pillows on which she is leaning, is the key to a new concept: Velázquez is not painting a Danae on a purple couch receiving Jupiter-rain of gold, nor a Leda between the wings of Jupiter-swan, nor a Venus regarding herself complacently in Jupiter-mirror; Velázquez is painting a naked woman reclining on her bed, surprised as she sits up, gathers her hair, looks in the mirror... He is painting a nude and nothing more, but for the first time in history.

Let us leaf through the yellowing pages of history, as absurd as the memory of a computer; perhaps not quite... When Velázquez arrived back in Madrid at the end of his first Italian journey, the count-duke, at the peak of his glory and popularity, was starting the construction of a modern palace worthy of his king; the palace of El Buen Retiro, which was built in 1635. Velázquez would contribute to its decoration with a series of equestrian portraits of the royal family for the sumptuous Hall of Realms. But, turning the page, in 1636, he was appointed assistant of the wardrobe; from here comes his wide knowledge of silks, satins, velvets, voiles, lace... which leads one to conclude that the *Venus of the Mirror* was painted in Madrid, before Velázquez set out on his second journey to Italy. For one reason, the dark, heavy, rustling silk, on which the naked beauty shines, is a typical Chinese silk. In Italy she would have reclined on velvets, or perhaps Oriental brocades brought from Persia... But neither before nor after Marco Polo were Chinese silks frequently seen in Italy. But in Madrid, yes, imported from the Philippines, the far end of the Spanish empire.

This traditional flow of imported Oriental products, basically Chinese, continued in Spain until the loss of her colonies in 1898. One of the most traditional elements of the Spanish wardrobe, the Manila shawl, obviously comes from these; originally these were Chinese shawls, imported via Manila until the beginning of this century. I remember that in my childhood there existed—or rather, persisted—in the old Madrid, I think in the street of Carretas near the Puerta del Sol, a shop called "Los Chinos" where this kind of product was to be found, principally silk stuffs; my grandparents, and my sisters as well, have dressed in *shantung* from "Los Chinos." The great farthingales of Philip IV's court were constructed—they really were constructions—from heavy, rustling Chinese silks; the childish farthingale worn by the Infanta Margarita, the sumptuous salmon pink and silver one she is portrayed in as an adolescent, the Infanta María Teresa's sand-pearl, the console-like farthingale, shown at her engagement on the Isle of Pheasants—in fact, all, except those which are obviously velvet, appear to have been fashioned from heavy Chinese silks—. The material of Velázquez' own costume on that ceremonial occasion, so eulogistically mentioned by Palomino many years later, must have been a heavy, rustling, dark Chinese silk. Perhaps too, the king's coffee and silver outfit in one of the most beautiful portraits of him from that time... (But let us cut short this interminable digression and zigzag back to the palace of El Buen Retiro, still unfinished).

The king, the younger friend, asked Velázquez to paint a series of pictures to decorate the sumptuous Hall of Realms in his new palace. And Velázquez painted—no less!—than the *Surrender of Breda*, the elegant and chivalrous "peace" of Breda, the picture known as *The Lances*, so far from the habitual Baroque glorifications of military victories, a picture in which the vanquished is sheltered under the hand of his armed conqueror who has respectfully bared his head before the humiliation and grief of the Burgomeister of Breda, not permitting him to kneel. Barely two years earlier, Rubens, in his series of tapestries for the convent of the Descalzas Reales, sends the triumphant Roman chariot of the church, pulled by wild beasts, rolling over the blood-stained dead and dying bodies of heretics and pagans. Velázquez has very different ideas about war and victory: about peace. Ideas as relevant today, as his painting, three centuries in advance of his time. (The conquering Marquis of Spínola seems to apologise; we are both guilty, victors and vanquished.)

He also painted for the Hall of Realms the three royal equestrian portraits; the king, the queen and the Prince Baltasar Carlos, the heir, and their three horses. Six characters not exactly in search of an author in this case... The image of the child rider has the symbolism of a Greek myth, the education of a young god. And great visual charm; the diminutive armour, the crimson sash across his chest, which waves in the wind from the Pardo, the white plumes in his hat... A charm which will last through the centuries. The picture's symbolic message and its attractive form reflect the king's deep love for his son and heir, both royal plaything and great hope for the future. Velázquez must have shared these feelings, analysing them as friend and mentor, during "those more exclusive hours" in the only Salon still showing a light in the sleeping Alcázar...

There is a curious picture, attributed to Velázquez—and probably by Velázquez—which records a scene in the little prince's equestrian education; the Count-Duke of Olivares himself, all-powerful Mars, is the instructor for the heir to the throne, the charming infant Apollo. From a palace balcony, Jupiter and Juno, the King and Queen—Jupiter the thunderer has left his thunderbolts leaning against the wall in a corner of the great balcony—, are watching the prince's progress from their Olympian distance... (But there is a very curious figure in the royal group; a little girl, beside the king and queen, who is clinging to the balcony rails to see better... Without doubt, this must be the Infanta María Teresa, the infanta absent from *Las Meninas*, and from the staircase of Las Descalzas, who was never portrayed again till Velázquez painted her with her long strings of pearls—the only pearls which Velázquez has painted!—her golden butterflies and her red and white court make-up, when her fate was decided and she was to be queen of France—the poor queen of France, cruelly relegated to second place by Louis XIV, behind his officially enthroned mistresses, that "third queen," unwitting key to an historic event which changed the world; the end of the Spanish House of Austria, the beginning of the end of the Spanish empire.)

The equestrian portrait of the queen is another story. Or, rather, the key to another story; the story of Velázquez' relations with the queen. In the enormous canvas in the Prado, the only portrait painted by Velázquez, the mentor, of his younger friend's wife, almost two thirds are not by Velázquez; moreover, the picture itself is "from Velázquez' workshop," with two sections undoubtedly by the hand of the great painter, the horse's head (which is really all that one can see of the noble creature, almost totally hidden under the queen's lavish robes) and the countryside through which it is passing. Practically two thirds of the canvas are taken up by these sumptuous robes, flat, lifeless, but meticulously precise in showing the rich quality of the cloth, the medieval style of the immense riding habit, the lace on its cuffs and at the neck, its embroideries, brooches, braid trimmings, buckles and buttons; its cut and workmanship and even the lining of its skirts. Furthermore, the queen's face, so high up, is blank and expressionless, like a cutting from a fashion plate, under the jewelled cap adorned with feathers, as minutely depicted as the enormous skirt which covers the enormous horse.

How is one to explain this absurd —and only—portrait of the queen, which was to be hung between the superb portraits of the king on horseback and the god-plaything, Prince Baltasar Carlos?

The absence of any portrait of the young queen, during the king's painters' first period in Madrid, can only be explained by the queen's marked indifference towards the young genius who had arrived from Seville. Indifference tinged with jealousy of "that nobody" whose influence over the king—because already he was usher to the bedchamber!—made itself felt even in the marriage bed. Paradoxically, Velázquez' long absence, during his first journey to Italy, increased the queen's jealousy. The king missed his elder friend more acutely every day. He did not know how, or did not dare, to live without him. When, at last, Velázquez returned, the king tried to improve relations between his mentor and his royal wife and asked him to paint *The*

*Coronation of the Virgin* for the queen's oratory. The picture was accepted with a courteous smile, but it was put in His Majesty's oratory.

The great project of decorating the palace of El Buen Retiro brought the king's painter, usher of the bed-chamber, again into contact with the queen, his sovereign mistress. Work on the palace began in 1635. In 1635, Velázquez was appointed assistant of the wardrobe. All the court dress and jewellery worn by the royal family passed through his hands. At about the same time he must have started to paint the equestrian portraits for the Hall of Realms. All this makes one think that the queen's riding habit could have produced a first confrontation between Her Majesty and Velázquez. The heavy splendour of the almost medieval apparel chosen by the queen was not exactly Velázquez' style, with his opaque Chinese silks. But the newly, or soon to be, appointed assistant of the wardrobe had to accept his mistress' commands with a polite bow, and the picture was begun…

Oh, no! The queen was not disposed to accept that so many hours of work and sleepless vigils should be rewarded by two brushstrokes for the glitter of a brooch and a few more to denote the skirt's shining border, embroidered with gold trimming. She, the queen, insisted that the brooch be visible and that one should be able to distinguish the design on the border of her dress. Her Majesty wished to impose "her fashion" even in the smallest details. At this the king's painter angrily dashed his "tablet of colours" to the ground. And the work was interrupted.

The queen went to the king with her story. The king, naturally, sided with his painter, something which the queen was unwilling to accept. Finally, a compromise solution was reached: An assistant, chosen by Velázquez would paint the dress. And so it was done. As the queen's figure and her enormous habit, which almost completely covers the horse, take up more than half the space of the picture, the portrait of the queen on horseback is, technically, "workshop of Velázquez."

I do not know the precise dates between which the equestrian portraits in the Hall of Realms were painted, so it is difficult for me to say with certainty whether Velázquez was given the post of assistant of the wardrobe before or after he painted them. On reflection, it seems more likely that it was afterwards, as a royal pat on the back from the king to his friend and mentor, so that, as well as being his painter and usher of his bedchamber, he could steer the court fashion away from the queen's vulgar and out-of-date French taste.

In any case, Velázquez completed the picture himself. It does not seem that either the queen's head or hands in this first and only portrait of her, from Velázquez' second period, are his own work. But, on the other hand, the portrait of the horse is undoubtedly by Velázquez... and what a Velázquez! The head of the splendid creature is indisputably one of the finest horse's heads ever painted. Velázquez must have shown it to the king with a great peal of laughter—a laugh from Seville, or rather, I was going to say, from Triana, its popular heart.

This court anecdote, invented to explain the absurdity of the picture in itself is, except in its details, historically true; the portrait of the queen on horseback symbolises the audacity with which Velázquez took another step, over the head of the queen, to secure the influence he had over the king. And for the elegant Philip IV, a great connoisseur, one more sign of his exceptional admiration for "his" painter; of the decisive influence which "his" painter would have on the history of painting. And more: on the history of universal culture.

It is curious to see a visible correction in the king's equestrian portrait. The horse seems about to launch itself with tremendous force over a possible dip in the rough ground of the Pardo's woodlands. But, today, the least observant visitor to the Prado can easily see that its forelegs have been repainted, corrected by Velázquez himself. There is a shadow over the landscape whose shape makes clear that, in the first version of the picture the horse was rushing forward with greater impetus. An impetus which was checked by Velázquez. A counsel of moderation to the eminent rider by his painter-mentor? In any case, the trace of the check can be seen without resort to radiography. And the correction itself is one more indication of the power of the reigned-in horse, dominated by his rider. With the same firmness with which he had just imposed the court fashion.

At around the same time, Velázquez painted the superb equestrian portrait of the Count-Duke of Olivares, to commemorate what was to be his last military triumph, the battle of Fuenterrabía. The count-duke appears overwhelmed by his own glory, everything about him is excessive; the plumes of his hat, the heavy, gleaming armour, the rod of all-powerful Mars, the triumphal gesture... Even the crimson sash barring his chest, which does not wave in the wind but falls heavily, weighed down by its magnificent border of sables. But his expression is mistrustful... A few years later, in 1643, having tumbled from political disaster to military disaster, the count-duke was forced by the king to resign from his office as Prime Minister and exiled to the town of Toro. R.I.P. But it was not in peace, but in despair, madness; oblivion.

The portrait of the *Royal Palfry with the queen* was hung in the Hall of Realms, facing *The Lances*, between the king on horseback and the young equestrian god, His Serene Highness, don Baltasar Carlos, prince of Spain, the Kingdom's hope... Velázquez' great peal of laughter was enshrined in the Hall of Realms in the palace of El Buen Retiro.

And the zigzagging evolution of Velázquez, now that he was relieved of all the traditional duties of a courtier by the clap on the back he had received from his Catholic Majesty, King Philip, took a new direction; the portrait as "portrait," the new style which would be the origin and precursor of the interminable series of portraits in modern painting: Goya, Manet, Renoir, Toulouse-Lautrec, Picasso... (Curiously, Ingres, who Picasso admired so deeply, does not seem to have descended from Velázquez, but from Zurbarán! The Ingres style, his original technique in the treatment of cloths and textures, which is essential and distinctive in his work, coincided with the remarkable exhibition of Zurbarán's paintings, organised by King Louis Philippe in the Palais Royale. Zurbarán was unknown in France until then, as was Velázquez. It appears that this great collection of Zurbaráns was part of the booty brought back to France by Napoleon's troops when they returned from Spain. And Zurbarán was, between white friar and white friar, the brilliant creator of the pictorial treatment of textiles, in their infinite combinations of colours and textures.)

The portraits with which Velázquez starts his series of portraits as "portrait" are the hunting portrait of the king, the little sporting Prince Baltasar Carlos, and the king's brother, the cardinal-infante, and their dogs. These portraits would decorate the Tower of the Parada, a small building, something between a fortified tower and a country retreat, in the heart of the Pardo forest, the extensive royal estate almost at the gates of Madrid, behind the palace of the Pardo, hunting lodge of the Hapsburg Kings, decorated with the two-headed imperial eagle of Charles V. (In my early youth I have seen foxes still hunted in the Pardo; the deer would flee in terror from the cars, while the rabbits gathered in their circular meeting places, absolutely indifferent to the forest guards and passers by.) Philip IV must have hunted deer, foxes, wild boars and bears in the Pardo; the coat-of-arms of Madrid, "town and court," is a bear standing on its hind legs, leaning against a strawberry tree... Altogether, in the 17th century, the Tower of the Parada —which still exists—must have been a much more private corner than the Alcázar. The hunting portraits were painted for this refuge. Perhaps it was this intimacy, this distance from the court and officialdom, the freedom which getting away from town can give, which liberated Velázquez from the strict rules of the official portrait, the portrait as identity card. And he wanted to fix with his brushes on the canvas not only how he saw his model, but what he, Velázquez, felt about him, and not only that, but what his model was thinking and feeling; the dreams—the life—of the person standing motionless in front of the great easel, the enigmatic rectangle of canvas with its back turned to him, on the other side of which, little by little, his image was being revealed... A psychiatric session where the "patient" did not lie nor did the "analyst" ask questions.

The official portrait, especially as regards the portraits of royal personages, was in the time of Velázquez, just that; a true international identity card, governed by rules as strict as are present-day passport photographs. Kings and princes appeared full-length and bare headed. Formerly, in the portraits of Charles V and Philip II by Titian and Pantoja de la Cruz, their heads were covered, the Emperor's with his jewelled caps, and the king's with his sober black hats. In the portraits of Philip IV, and those of his sons and brothers, they are always shown bareheaded, though their hats are always present as well: on a desk, in their hand, on pillows in the case of the princely children. Even the little Prince Felipe Próspero has a monumental velvet cap adorned with plumes and ermine, resting on a cushion with gold tassels, a hat which the fragile heir to the empire would have found difficult to wear. But this ever-present hat had a symbolic meaning; the king, the princes and the infantes of Spain were not obliged "to take off their hat to anyone," as the saying was... (The poor gentleman in *El Lazarillo de Tormes*, a picaresque novel, left his village for the court, abandoning his house and dovecotes, "for nothing more than not taking off his hat to one of his neighbours.") Why then were the Kings and princes no longer wearing them in their portraits? Probably it was due to something more hypersensitive than a weathercock—the caprice of fashion; the hats, which were "the thing" in the 17th century had become large, with wide brims which intentionally hid part of the face, already shadowed by the drooping plumes which overhung the hat itself. And as in today's passports, in official portraits the likeness was essential.

One of the companions of the Duke of Gramont, marshal of France and occasional ambassador extraordinary to Philip IV, remarks in his travel notes: "The king of Spain was dressed very simply and his aspect was exceedingly like one of his portraits." An indirect compliment to Velázquez, because the king, alone under a large canopy, was, besides, wearing a hat, although the French courtier does not tell us whether it was wide-brimmed and with plumes; it must have had a brim because he adds: "When the marshal came into the room, the king raised his hand to his hat," but did not take it off: How precisely measured Spanish courtesy was in the 17th century!

All this goes to show the new spirit of the hunting portraits. The king, Prince Baltasar Carlos and the cardinal-infante are wearing their hunting caps. But...

A copy exists of the portrait of Philip IV hunting, in which he is holding the cap in his left hand, which is resting against his hip. In the original in the Prado, the king wears his hunting cap and his left hand hangs freely at his side. Apart from the cap off or the cap on, the two pictures—the original in the Prado and its replica—are exactly the same. But…

If one studies the marvellous original portrait in the Prado carefully, one can see, with the naked eye, that there is a shadow beside the king's left hand, which is the same shape as the cap which, in the replica, he holds in his hand. A shadow similar, though less clear, to the one next to the horses forelegs in the equestrian portrait of the king. Which raises the possibility that, in the first version of the king's portrait, His Catholic Majesty was bareheaded, in accordance with the established norms for royal portraits. Velázquez felt freer when portraying the little prince and the cardinal-infante and left them just as they were, with their caps on, when they walked in the Pardo. This seemed an excellent idea to the sensitive critic, which the king really was; he saw their portraits as being more "true" than his own. And his painter, delighted, put the elegant cap back on his head. Did it really happen like that? The radiograph can give the answer. Another excellent and sensitive critic, the great Palomino, brings out that fresh atmosphere in the hunting portraits; the feeling of being "at home," of unwitnessed intimacy which they give—intended as they were for the Tower of the Parada—for the first time in the history of portraiture. This is what Palomino says:

> Don Diego Velázquez also painted two portraits, one of His Catholic Majesty, our lord don Philip IV, the other of his brother, His serene Highness don Ferdinand of Austria, from nature, on foot, dressed for hunting with their guns in their hands and their dogs on the leash, resting. It seems that he saw them at the hottest time of day, arriving tired from the exercise of hunting, which is as arduous as it is delightful, in graceful disarray, their hair powdered with dust, (not what courtiers use today) their faces bathed in sweat, as Martial describes Domitian, beautiful with sweat and dust, in a similar case, and Diego Velázquez could imitate many other poets who ex-

plain how much grace is added to beauty by weariness and dishevelment, an air of negligence.

Nevertheless, the tradition of the official portrait was so strong that the three royal personages still retain their conventional attitude in front of the painter. But not so their dogs; now they are no longer like the great dogs or hieratic lions in the portraits by Titian or Sánchez Coello; each one freely takes up the position which befits his character; this big fellow rests and snores with his muzzle against the ground; the other, as thin as if made of wire, alert and tense, sniffs the air and pricks its ears; another looks at us impassively; he has nothing against stags and wild boars and the shots bother him: Thank God the hunt is over!

Velázquez must have felt the contrast, the evident difference between the dogs "who seem to speak" and their eminent masters, who jealously keep their secrets. The order in which the portraits were painted would have been dictated by protocol; first, that of the king, then the Crown Prince's and, last of all, that of the cardinal-infante. And it is curious that the one who seems most free, in the position he has taken up, is this last, the complex and sagacious cardinal-infante; he has just halted and it seems as if his clothes are still moving to the rhythm of his steps, or had been moving only seconds before. He has the attitude which really corresponds to the man he was: As a youth, cardinal archbishop of Toledo, primate of Spain; shortly afterwards, victorious general and astute politician in Naples and Flanders. (In Flanders, acting as the king's agent in the acquisition of works of art, the young cardinal-infante resisted some conscientious objections to the purchase of Rubens' splendid nudes, *The Three Graces,* too naked for the austere intimacy of the young cardinal's quarters, but which finally took the place of honour which they deserved, in the royal collection in Madrid's Alcázar. In the forest of the Pardo, don Fernando of Austria becomes again the young infante who smilingly accepts, with his innate grace, the caprices of his elder brother, still so young, His Catholic Majesty, King Philip, and of his mentor, painter and usher of the bedchamber, also young.) But the, officially, silent painter and usher of the bedchamber must have thought, with a sigh, that, no, it would still not be possible to paint the king gazing into the distance, with his gloved hand absently twirling the tips of his gold moustache; nor the little prince in the Pardo, far away from his watchful governess—a respectable Spanish grandee—biting the fingertip of his small hunter's glove, so as to tear it off with a single tug and "throw down the gauntlet" like a grown man!

The two great canvases, *Esop* and *Menippus* were also painted for the Tower of the Parada; the presence of the Greek fabulist in the Pardo forest is justified by the abundance of game—birds, rabbits and so on, protagonists of his fables. The absence of a computer's memory prevents me from accounting for the presence there of Menippus, who must have been another Greek, more or less bucolic. At any rate, in Velázquez' posthumous portraits of them, these illustrious personages are personified by two wandering alcoholics, two *clochards,* not from the wharfs and bridges of the Parisian Seine, but vagabonds from the sandy shores of Madrid's Manzanares. Two big portraits, full length and of natural size, with dark backgrounds, which have acquired an unjustified popularity among Velázquez' works, comparable to that of *The Triumph of Bacchus;* perhaps because they were considered to be two topers, lost in the Pardo, who did not arrive in time to the triumph of *The Topers?*

Shortly before or after this, Velázquez had painted his first buffoons, his first jesters: *Pablillo de Valladolid* and *Don*

*Juan of Austria.* Both, like *Esop* and *Menippus*, are portraits conceived within the tradition of the official portrait, with some freedom of attitude, and Menippus and don Juan of Austria are wearing their hats! Starting from these four initial portraits, there begins an extraordinary series of dwarfs and buffoons. In their form there is one fundamental innovation; they are always smaller than Velázquez' traditional portraits and those of others in his time —the 17th century—; a norm which Velázquez first accepted and from which he broke away, definitively, in his series of portraits of dwarfs and buffoons. They are all full-length and all of varying size, but always much smaller than the usual one, that of *Esop* and *Don Juan of Austria.* This intimacy of feeling and flexibility of form, always in accordance with the character of the person portrayed and the atmosphere that surrounds him, originate with Velázquez; and are fundamental characteristics of the modern portrait, which would last until Picasso (think of his portraits of Gertrude Stein and Dora Maar) because they imply a new concept of painting; the pictorial expression of what is not seen. Part of this invisible but present world can be detected in the attitude of the sitter—in the position he freely takes up, his involuntary expression; of timidity, boldness, aggression or indifference towards his painter, or today, towards his photographer—. But, of course, Velázquez surpassed the "candid camera." Because Velázquez reveals, at the same time as he paints, his contempt, his repugnance, his compassion, his own judgement on his fascinating models. One only needs to review the series of his buffoons or lunatics. One of them, *Calabazas,* is still today, from the psychological point of view, one of the best portraits in the world. As a portrait and as a picture. Which is to say, illustrious and admirable Palomino, as "truth" and as "painting."

## THE GREAT "TRUTH" ARRIVES IN ROME

In 1643, Velázquez was chosen by the king to "assist" in the superintendence of private works, a new royal favour which, as Palomino says "seems to wear the guise of punishment." The new "curator" of the royal collections used his free time as the king's painter, which had become increasingly free with each day that passed, for the work. But, one day, Velázquez unexpectedly decided to abandon Madrid and the court and to return to Italy, to Rome; perhaps to go on to Paris. The king immediately authorized, justified and financed the travel plans of his new superintendent of private works. And in November, 1648, Velázquez started on his second journey to Italy. Only a few months later, in 1649, Philip IV married the fourteen-year-old archduchess, Mariana of Austria, who had been the promised bride of Prince Baltasar Carlos. But his friend and mentor did not wish to be present during the solemn bridal ceremonies for the new queen. Why?

Velázquez must have arrived at a critical juncture in his life. He needed solitude, isolation, time to think, under a different sky. He had not finished painting his first and only female nude, the first "nude" in history, the so-called *Venus of the Mirror*. And, nevertheless, he packed his palette, his new pigments—natural carmines, extracted from a caterpillar, American cochineal from Mexico—his long-stemmed paintbrushes, the fine and the thick, and he left! The *Venus* was given to don Luis de Haro, the king's new prime minister, a nephew of the count-duke, upon Velázquez' return to Spain. This has given rise to the idea that the picture might have been painted in Italy. But the model seems to be a slender, dark and modest Spanish beauty, reclining on Chinese silk, brought to Madrid from the Philippines. Isn't it possible that the hardly visible black veil, which she holds against her heart with her left hand and with which she is trying to cover herself, was the mantilla in which the mysterious *Lady with a Fan* was going to mass? Her face in the mirror, like the faces of Goya's "Majas," is a mask, barely sketched. But the nude is a portrait, as much a portrait as *The Lady with a Fan*, which many have thought to be a portrait of the painter's daughter. (Both suppositions are compatible, though not frequent: Rubens' *Three Graces* which hangs in the Prado, obtained for the royal collection by the cardinal-infante, is a triple nude portrait of the painter's second wife, Helena Fourmet, in which the faces are hardly differentiated or disguised.)

Spain, like Velázquez, had reached a critical moment in her history; the Count-Duke of Olivares, whom Velázquez had met at the height of his glory, had tumbled from the glossy warhorse of all-powerful Mars with a great crash of his shining armour, dented in the fall, and entangled in his silk and sable sash, never to rise again from his exile in Toro; to be replaced by his nephew, don Luis de Haro, in the post of His Majesty's prime minister.

In the new palace of El Buen Retiro, surrounded by parks and gardens, fountains, pools, gondolas and summer pavilions... His Catholic Majesty King Philip found himself painfully alone, more desolate with each passing day. He had lost the queen; his brother, the cardinal-infante, had also died and, unexpectedly, the charming Prince Baltasar Carlos, pride of the court and hope for the future—dead when only seventeen!—. The king found himself absolutely alone; and, alone too in the children's quarters was his daughter María Teresa, a poor mentally retarded girl, kept apart by duennas, attendants and guards... But, in the most private hours, the king would shut himself away with Velázquez in the office room; with his friend and mentor, who was more profoundly solitary than his sovereign and junior: Historically, this companionship, this shared life under the same roof for thirty years, can only be compared to the classical and mythical friendship of Pylades and Orestes. The king and Velázquez; two solitaries through pride. Hereditary pride on the king's part; he was the most powerful monarch on Earth. Pride in Velázquez through self-esteem; he was conscious of being the greatest artist of his time. The king and Velázquez; two solitaries through pride. Two inseparable solitaries. The king had said, when he was eighteen, on meeting Velázquez: "Only Velázquez." And Velázquez at twenty-four, bending to kiss the king's hand: "Nobody but the king." The king and Velázquez; two proud twin souls, two inseparable solitaries. The explanation for this mutual admiration, this fraternal affection, this curious shared solitude throughout a lifetime under the same roof, must be somewhere in Freud. (Some day we will look for it.) But, in the most unbearably dramatic moments of the king's life, Velázquez, his only friend, abandons him.

In the last years of their shared life, probably during the months of mourning for the death of the Crown Prince, a decisive event took place in the king's life; the official recognition of his bastard son, from his liaison with a beautiful and popular actress, la Calderona. The boy had been born in the same year as Prince Baltasar Carlos, 1629, a love child, not the child of dynastic duty, and, it appears, as handsome, as charming, as intelligent, as his brother, the prince. His father, the king, became fond of this other unwanted and splendid toy, who would escape from the little patio of his mother's house, whose flower pots Lope de Vega would have tended and Calderón disdained, to run all over Madrid; to las Cavas (the cellars), la calle de la Pasa (street of the raisin), la plaza de la Cebada (Barley Square), la calle de don Pedro... without nurses, without stewards, without ushers of the bedchamber, alone, like a sunbeam lost in a labyrinth. The king paid attention to his education; the all-powerful count-duke did not, so far as we know, take charge of his riding lessons, but he had his own ponies and his aristocratic little riding boots. Velázquez did not paint him, but he, too, had his miniature shotgun, his hunting cap, his gauntlets, his dogs and his schoolbooks. And his voluminous Latin grammar, which perhaps the cardinal-infante would look over with him. After the death of Prince Baltasar Carlos, la Calderona's son was, without question, the most dazzling young gallant in the town and court. His father, the king, dazzled like everyone else, gave him his surname and presented him at court; the son of la Calderona was transformed overnight into don John of Austria, an historic and turbulent second don John of Austria; to start with, dean of the Military Order of Saint John; in later years, Prince of the Sea, supreme head of the Spanish navy.

Boosted by his worldly and military success, the Prince of the Sea repeatedly petitioned his father to grant him the title of Royal Highness, infante of Spain. But this His Catholic Majesty—perhaps because of his Catholicism—continued to refuse him up to his death. And, instead, he decided to remarry, to fulfil his dynastic duty, to leave an heir born in the Alcázar, in the royal bed in the queen's bedchamber, and not in the maze of little streets in lower Madrid, in that room with its little patio full of flower pots, and a background of curtains painted with gods, kings and crowns, lit by flickering oil lamps.

Did this decision of the king's have any bearing on Velázquez' temporary absence, which could have been definitive? In any case, Velázquez felt an instinctive antipathy towards the two Queens, Isabella of Bourbon and Mariana of Austria; the wives of his friend. It is enough to look objectively at his work, which is his life, and correlate it with the meagre and bare historical data of his years in Madrid, a record of no interest by itself. The only portrait, let us say "by Velázquez," of Queen Isabella of Bourbon, the portrait of the queen on horseback, and the historical date of Velázquez' appointment as assistant of the wardrobe, confirms the situation at the heart of the emotional triangle king-Velázquez-queen, his scornful attitude towards his sovereign mistress, his hostility, even, to that commonplace and dense Frenchwoman and the king's partiality for his painter. Velázquez exerted an emotional dominance over the king which was nothing to do with his position as courtier. The relations between Velázquez and the king, the two inseparable solitaries, sprang from much deeper sources.

Velázquez did not want to be present at the king's wedding to his niece, Mariana of Austria. And this time he resolved the question with two strokes;

the first, his absence; the second, his superb and only portrait of the Queen Mariana of Austria; hidden inside her voluminous, stiff and solemn Velazquean farthingale like a snail inside its shell. And not another brushstroke, God willing!

On the other hand, he showed an almost paternal tenderness towards the children of his friend, the king, a tenderness which he does not seem to have felt for his own daughters. It is sufficient to run through the series of portraits of Prince Baltasar Carlos, the son of Isabella of Bourbon and the dazzling collection of pictures of the Infanta Margarita, first-born daughter of Mariana of Austria, up until her glorification in *Las Meninas*, now dressed like a little woman in her diminutive farthingale;

the frail heiress to the greatest empire which the world had known. This little infanta is really an enchanting personification of the dynasty, the centre of the most powerful and elegant court in the world; court and power not to be seen in the refined austerity of the gallery in the prince's quarters, where *la serenísima infanta*, five years old, alone, personifies, and will personify through the centuries, the end of the Spanish house of Austria: The Golden Age, beginning of the end of the Spanish empire.

But, before painting *Las Meninas*, Velázquez had gone away, in November 1648, leaving the king completely alone in his Alcázar in Madrid and his palace of El Buen Retiro. He was, for the second time, on his way to Italy. And the great "truth," whose secret he alone possessed —although perhaps he did not yet know it—arrived in Rome.

## TWO WINDOWS OPEN ON THE GREAT "TRUTH"

The two windows are the two landscapes of the Villa Medici in Rome which Velázquez painted during his second Italian journey, between November 1648 and July 1651. He brought them in his luggage when he arrived in Madrid in the summer of 1651. The Infanta Margarita was about to be born or had just been born. The two extraordinary landscapes are two very small pictures, the perfect size for an apartment today;

two landscapes painted for the 20th century!

The difference in size between the two pairs of pictures which Velázquez brought to Madrid after his two Italian journeys is curious, remarkable, and so we remark on it here; the two enormous canvases, *Vulcan's Forge* and *Joseph's Brothers* after his first journey and the two small landscapes of the Villa Medici after his second. They indicate his personal evolution towards a greater intimacy, a direction he had begun to take in his portraits of dwarfs and buffoons. Moreover, his last portrait of the king, contemporary with *Las Meninas*, is not much bigger in size than the two landscapes; showing no more than the king's head above the white, horizontal line of his collar, starched and flat according to the fashion at the time; an isolated, living head, placed like the severed head of John the Baptist on a plate... (The best portrait of the king ever painted by Velázquez.)

What emotion must his friend, the king, have felt on opening the box placed on a table in his painter's workshop!.. (Whose key, as Pacheco has told us, he had kept ever since Velázquez, as the king's painter, installed his workshop in the Alcázar; and as Velázquez had carried at his waist the key to the royal bedchamber, since his appointment, some years later, as usher of the bedchamber.) The king opened the box, like someone opening a great mother-of-pearl shell, and extracted the two small canvases, two "perfect pearls," remarkable for their iridescent beauty, and for their size! (The famous *perla Peregrina*, fished in the Caribbean, and never surpassed for its lustre and size, had reached the hands of Philip III half a century earlier.)

Velázquez probably painted the two landscapes of the "Medicis' vineyard" as Palomino terms it, in the open air, with his easel firmly planted in the sand of the garden. He painted first the façade of the Grotto-loggia, under repair at the time, covered with planks. But no breeze stirred the slender tops of the cypresses, the trimmed box gave out no scent, like the scent of the hedges in the Friar's Garden in El Escorial, when they are warmed by the afternoon sun... There was something dead, distant, from another world—the world of "painting"—in the very beautiful, freshly painted landscape: *The Grotto-Loggia of the Medicis* was still more "painting" than "truth"—to use Palomino's expressive phrase—. And the temperamental Velázquez seized his easel and planted it in front of the pavilion of Cleopatra-Ariadna, a great portico opening inside the garden onto the garden, and brought out his long brushes "the fine and thick brushes which he sometimes used to paint at a greater distance and with such mastery that from close it could not be understood and from far it is a miracle" as the same Palomino relates. Half an hour later, the miracle was completed.

The true miracle is the time that separates these two landscapes, these two "windows" which are beginning to open on the great "truth"; half an hour, a day, a week, a month? Because in the evolution of any painter, any great painter, the step from the first to the second of the Villa Medici landscapes—perhaps painted on the same afternoon—would usually take twenty or twenty-five years of work. Perhaps Velázquez—he was a cerebral painter—took the same time, twenty or twenty-five years of speculation. From *The Water Seller of Seville* to the *Venus of the Mirror.* But the speed of speculation in Velázquez cannot be measured by the hands of a clock. The *Grotto-Loggia* is contemporary, with Vermeer's *View of Delft*, which Proust considered the greatest picture in the world. Curiously, Velázquez knew nothing of Vermeer, nor did Vermeer know about Velázquez, two great artists absolutely contemporary and profoundly akin. Perhaps this was due to the political and military differences between Spain and Holland, perhaps to the conservative taste of the cardinal-infante, so different from that of Philip IV, that discriminating and revolutionary Diaghilev of the 17th century... To return to the Villa Medici, what is surprising, extraordinary, miraculous even, is that the second landscape, *The Pavilion of Cleopatra-Ariadna* could be contemporary with Van Gogh's *The Starry Night,* another great painter with a profound affinity to Velázquez: Velázquez has travelled more than two centuries in less than twenty years, perhaps in the last twenty minutes.

In the gallery of the former home of Prince Baltasar Carlos, the two landscapes opened like two windows onto the

Medicis' vineyard. But the light which inundates the *Pavilion of Cleopatra-Ariadna* comes through the arch of the pavilion in the background and passes through the picture. And here is one of the most evident aspects of the discovery of the "truth" which has now definitively ceased to be "painting." This path of light in the background is present in all the pictures of Velázquez' final period; the half-open door behind *Las Meninas:*

> At the left side of the mirror there is an open door, which gives onto a staircase on which José Nieto, *aposentador* to the queen, is standing, very recognisable, in spite of the distance and diminution of size and of light in which he is seen.

This is how Palomino describes the first view of things seen against the light in the history of painting; the great stream of light falling on Arachne's workshop in *The Weavers*, the patch of light behind Mercury, who is dragging himself along—the god who, before Velázquez, had always flown, now without his staff and wearing a wretched felt hat with two pigeons' wings sewn into its sides instead of his shining winged helmet—in the superb *Mercury and Argos.*

In 1652, the king appointed Velázquez *aposentador mayor de Palacio,* the last position which he held in the court until his death in 1660. In these few years, Velázquez converted Madrid's disorderly Alcázar into something unique in the world. The painter and courtier was not a "courtier," he was a technician, in this case, we would say today, an extraordinary decorator.

Jonathan Brown cites a contemporary witness to his success as a decorator. On the 16th of October, 1659, the Marshal-Duke of Gramont, ambassador extraordinary of Louis XIV, arrived in Madrid; he had come to ask the hand in marriage of the Infanta María Teresa for the king of France.

"Two members of the French party later described the event," says Brown "and a collage of these events reveals the impact of the Hall of Mirrors and the ceremony on the foreign visitors":

> We passed through a number of rooms with wainscoting which were full of pictures... And, having walked through galleries and Salons full of statues, we finally arrived in a large room where the king was waiting (the Hall of Mirrors).

> The king of Spain was wearing a very simple costume and greatly resembled his portraits. He was standing beneath a very rich canopy at the end of the room. There was no one near him. Above the top of the canopy was the portrait of Charles V, done by Titian, which was so lifelike that I believed the horse and rider were still alive.

As we have seen, "When the Marshal entered the room the king raised his hand to his hat. And he did not change position when the Marshal handed him the letter."

"Lack of space, of dramatic feeling, of delicacy," is how Brown judges the first portrait of Philip IV, the source of the magnificent spectacle offered to the French. And the admiring Frenchman concludes: "Although the dress of the

Spaniard was not among the most brilliant, there was nevertheless an air of grandeur and majesty which I have never seen equalled." And they had come straight from Versailles!

This description of the historic ceremony seems like a scenic realisation of the indelible impression which Velázquez took away from his first meeting with the king. An impression which fundamentally changed his life, and his life, we insist, was his work. The, by then, *aposentador mayor*, decorator of genius, created from a few elements—Titian's superb portrait of Charles V on horseback—an enormous canopy of great richness, a series of heavy mirrors, those key mirrors in *Las Meninas* and the *Venus*—an image of the solitary grandeur of the king of Spain. His

Catholic Majesty, served and obeyed from a distance by a silent court of sombre gentlemen—such as those seen in El Greco's wonderful *Burial of the Count of Orgaz*. All this crowned with Titian's portrait, an anti-heraldic symbol of empire. (We should not forget that Velázquez—when still "our" Velázquez of Seville—removed the laurel crown, traditional symbol of glory, from the brow of the glorious Góngora.)

But his pictures are, in their turn, enhanced by his professional experiences, architectural and decorative. To begin with, his two Villa Medici landscapes are two studies of architecture. Visualising one of them, Velázquez realises the importance of the light, which comes from behind in his picture, as one needs to take light into account in any architectural project to judge its viability. In *The Weavers*, the light, which floods into the background of the picture shows an architectural cross section of Arachne's workshop very precisely reproduced, and exactly completed when Velázquez enlarged the canvas.

*Las Meninas* too can be seen in a certain way as the cross-section of an architectural plan in which the figures serve to calculate the true dimensions of the space they occupy. Only the clarity of the great balcony on the right and above all, the hatchet of light from the open door to the staircase at the back, transform the "plan," the painted canvas, the picture, into life. Palomino was the first to note it: "It is not painting, it is truth." But the illustrious Acisclo Antonio Palomino, perhaps because he was too close in time, because he lacked perspective or, in this instance, perspicacity, did not remove the guise of punishment from the king's magnanimity and did not realise what Velázquez the painter owes to Velázquez, assistant of the private works and *aposentador mayor* of the palace. Illustrious Palomino: The king knew very well what he was doing when without "disguise of punishment" he placed the red cross of Santiago on the black doublet of the man who had painted *Las Meninas*, symbolic glorification of a career which he had directed so skilfully; that of the painter and not the courtier.

In the year 1660, Velázquez unexpectedly died in his home in Madrid's Alcázar. He had arrived at court some weeks earlier, on return from his official visit to the Isle of Pheasants where, according to Palomino, he had distinguished himself by his personal grace, his courteous manners and his elegance. He continued to be the eternally young painter of his self-portrait in *Las Meninas*. About a year later, Prince Felipe Próspero dies, just before his fourth birthday. The melancholy prophesy illustrated in *Las Meninas*—the touching close to a whole glorious epoch, whose only heir is a little girl of five—returns, like a deep sigh, to fill the room of the king's office... But the last heir is born, Prince Carlos, Charles II. Philip IV dies in 1665. And, in 1700, Charles II, "the bewitched" dies without descendents, when the Infanta Margarita, Empress of Austria has died already. The prophesy has been fulfilled; the melancholy end of the Austrias, the beginning of the end of the Spanish empire.

## THE KIDNAPPING OF THE GREAT "TRUTH"

Once Velázquez was dead, Velázquez was buried; by which, I mean, his works. Until 1700, while the House of Austria still ruled, Velázquez' paintings remained in the Alcázar. But those who, like Palomino, were able to gain access to the court were very few. Added to this, Velázquez had his studio, but never his school. His ever-changing manner could neither be copied nor inherited, nor could his genius be passed on. Perhaps the only man "of the school of

Velázquez" was Philip IV, who didn't paint!

With the Bourbons, from 1700 onwards, Velázquez' work, that great "truth," was jealously hidden. For two reasons, the first political, the Austrian past had to be erased. With cannon fire on Spanish soil and at the bottom of the most dismal basement in the court of Madrid. The second reason, more frivolous and so more compelling, was fashion; with the wigs of the Bourbons, the life style of Versailles arrived in Madrid. The austere room of the king's office was closed up with stones and mortar. In its shadowy depths, *Las Meninas* became the cave of Altamira of modern art. The providential, or rather, opportune, fire in the old Alcázar was a decisive stylistic turning point.

How could they hang *Las Meninas* over the *chinoiseries* of the Salon of Porcelain in the new Palacio de Oriente? Furthermore, to the great French and Italian masters, Mengs, Tiepolo and their followers, who frequented the new Madrid, *Las Meninas* must have seemed an abominable picture, the *Demoiselles d'Avignon* of their time. Nevertheless, there is a judgement by Mengs on Velázquez which is worth bringing out. I quote from Jonathan Brown:

> But where, without doubt, he gave the most accurate idea of the natural is in the painting of *The Weavers*, which is of his last style, and done in such a way as it seems as if the hand played no part in the execution, but that he painted it only as an act of will.

Will; thought, reason, mind. Mengs is the first painter—in this case, the first critic—after Velázquez, who considers the great painter who preceded him as a cerebral painter. As, obviously Mengs had not read Palomino, it did not enter his head to classify him so erroneously as "painter and courtier." This of course, Mengs himself was. But, precisely because of this, he saw Velázquez as a special painter, "a case apart," a theoretician, a "theorem painter," mistaken and a genius.

Years later, how did Goya, himself a court painter, manage to see Velázquez' pictures in the new Palacio de Oriente? Apparently, nearly all of the Velázquez now in the Prado is listed in the inventories of the new palace, but naturally the inventories don't specify where they were hung. Goya must have looked repeatedly through the enormous storerooms of the palace, where the superb heritage of the Austrias was stacked, and discovered Velázquez, as Pompei had just been discovered!

Velázquez was buried for over a century under the lava of oblivion, an atrocious political kidnapping. In any case, Goya is the first great painter to have admired Velázquez. Without having seen *Las Meninas* and the *Venus of the Mirrors* he would never have painted his court portraits—*The Family of the Infante don Luis* and the *Family of Charles IV*—nor his *Majas.* But, as Goya was not cerebral, but passionate and direct, he does not pause to consider the mirrors in the two Velázquez portraits. Result: What is Goya painting at his two big easels with their backs turned to the public of his two great court portraits? And what is the *Maja Desnuda* doing, naked on her bed? (Although the *Maja* is waiting with her eyes fixed on her bedroom door, which is not seen in any mirror, to see who is coming in. All too obviously, Goya paints, sure that the *Maja* is waiting for him. But, today, the one who enters through that unseen bedroom door, is you or me, or any tourist with a reasonable supply of euros… What is she to do?)

At all events, with the end of the Spanish Austrias, the Velázquezs disappear, the great "truth" is kidnapped. Our friend the Duke of Saint-Simon is, by omission, an exceptional witness to this historical fact. In 1721, Saint-Simon travelled to Spain as ambassador extraordinary of the Duke of Orleans, regent of France during the minority of Louis XV, great grandson and heir of Louis XIV, to arrange two royal weddings, that of Louis XV, the nine-year-old king of France with a little Spanish infanta, aged four, daughter of the first Bourbon King, Philip V; and that of the then Prince of Asturias with mademoiselle de Montpensier, daughter of the regent, both adolescents. The two marriage contracts were officially signed in one of the salons of Madrid's old Alcázar, which Velázquez had decorated. The marriage ceremony of the Prince of Asturias was celebrated in the palace of the Duke of Lerma, Philip III's unpopular prime minister, in the town of Lerma, near Segovia. At the insistence of the French, the consummation of the marriage had to be simulated, in front of a whole court of astonished Spaniards. The Duke of Saint-Simon, organizer of the project—the newly-weds were still too young for a real consummation—recounts the event in his memoirs in great detail. With the same wealth of detail with which he describes and relates everything that he saw and did in Madrid. In his description of the old Alcázar, and the ceremonies which took place there, he does not omit the smallest point; the splendour of the old building, the quality of the carpets, the clothes and the placement of the personages there (with plans drawn by himself, rather badly), the magnificent carriage horses, the discomfort of the carriages, the capes of the coachmen and grooms, the red cushions on which the ladies sat in the palace salons, of velvet or satin according to their rank... (Because the court ladies still followed the custom established when the Velazquean farthingale was worn, the court uniform in which they could not sit, even in the big chairs against which they leant for their state portraits and "took the cushion" when they were received as ladies-in-waiting.) With the same exactitude and minuteness he describes his first official visit to the king.

The first Bourbon king received him in the Hall of Mirrors, as Philip IV had received the Marshal-Duke of Gramont, about fifty years earlier, under a great canopy, but the Emperor Charles V, painted by Titian, is no longer advancing on horseback. Saint-Simon does not mention a single picture in his descriptions of the Alcázar; and *Las Meninas* would not have passed unnoticed before his discerning gaze! But he does mention—alas!—the size and lustre of the *perla Peregrina*, which adorned the hat of Philip V of Bourbon—in exactly the same way as it had adorned that of Philip III of Austria—at the ball in Madrid, held to celebrate the wedding of the Duke of Lerma. The absence of Velázquez and the reappearance of the *perla Peregrina* are symbolic of the political life of Spain during the 18th century. But, neither from oral nor literary accounts, do we know where the great "truth" was hidden, or exhibited.

Unexpectedly, there is a mention of Velázquez in the National Episodes, by Galdós, the great writer of the 19th and early 20th centuries. I seem to remember that it is in *Los duendes de la camarilla*, one of the episodes of the final series, where Galdós describes how Ferdinand VII met up with his cronies at a typical café gathering, where the famous Pepa, "the orange seller," was one of the shining lights, but that this took place in the palace, in his office with its silk-covered walls and gilded furniture, presided over by Velázquez' *The Topers*! True or not, the picture is a curious one. Ferdinand VII was the king who installed the whole magnificent royal collection of paintings in the beautiful building of the Prado of San Jerónimo, up until then the National History Museum, creating, in 1819, the present day Prado Museum.

In 1819, the new Prado Museum, then called "the Royal Gallery," opened its doors to the great "truth." And to the Spanish people who, for the first time, would be able to admire the superb collection of the Austrian rulers. But, after the disasters of the war, which Goya lived through and depicted, the Spaniards were not ready to visit museums. *Las Meninas* remained for long years in solitude, forgotten in the depths of the room in the Prado where they were traditionally displayed, as they had been after the death of Philip IV, alone at the end of the king's office in the old Alcázar, afterwards destroyed by fire (guarded by the usher of the bedchamber on duty, who, in the Prado, became a plain "usher").

Very few too were the foreigners who arrived in Madrid, having dared to travel, in the shabby Spanish stage-coaches, on horseback or on foot, through the roads infested with brigands of a wretched and unsettled Spain. The French Romantics were the first to discover this new Spain, proud, hungry and ransacked; despite the Spanish people's hatred of the French, having suffered, bodily, the disasters of the war against Napoleon, as Goya shows us in his engravings and paintings. This war of independence was in part a civil war, in which the progressive and Frenchified Goya, voluntarily exiled in France, had himself suffered. It was the romantic explosion of a whole people, whose sudden blaze seared the eyelashes and fired the hearts of writers and artists on the other side of the Pyrenees. Because of this, the first articulate cry of French Romanticism, the opening performance of Victor Hugo's *Hernani* in the *Comédie Française* in Paris in 1830, is a Spanish shout; Hernani, the heroine's name in the famous play, is that of a little town in the Spanish Basque country; the drama unfolds in 16th-century Spain, the passions are Spanish; rebellious love, unyielding nobles, hatred and loyalty... (Another link with the Spanish war of independence: the opening performance of *Hernani* has passed into history as "the battle of Hernani," the final victory over the still latent, imperial and neo-classical spirit of the Corsican Bonaparte.) Hugo had lived in Spain as a child; his father was an officer in Napoleon's invading army. I quote from memory—insisting that one's own recollections are more authentic than a filing card or the memory of a computer—a piece of verse, hardly even a line, from a poem, almost a song, of Victor Hugo's, in which he evokes his childhood days in barbarous Spain. Some peasant women are walking across country to their village; some black fighting bulls approach in a cloud of dust... and *le petit* Hugo cries out in alarm: "Cachez vos rouges tabliers!"... Victor Hugo carried Spain in his memory, which, as we all know today, is, in various forms ineffaceable, as much a part of us as our bones. Gautier, Mérimée, George Sand, Chopin, Dumas, and many others, travelled in Spain, among them, by now in the mid-19th century, Manet.

The great Manet, is the discoverer of Velázquez—re-discoverer in fact, because the prime discoverer was Philip IV—. Velázquez must have impressed Manet as deeply as the young painter from Seville had impressed the youthful king. Manet has left us his judgement; He is *le peintre des peintres.* The king too, over forty years, through that series of royal appointments, that string of "rewards which appear to wear the guise of punishment," as Palomino tells us, confirmed it throughout his life. For many years, in picture after picture, Manet paints his admiration for *le peintre des peintres;* and the previously unknown Velázquez becomes the great *maître* of modern painting. He rated him above Goya, a century and a half more modern than him. Because it seems more than likely that Manet went to Madrid in search of Goya, *le formidable* Spanish painter, voluntarily exiled in Bordeaux, where he painted some of his best pictures—personally, I would say, his best picture—the wonderful *Milkmaid of Bordeaux*, and where he died. In Madrid, Manet saw *The Family of Charles IV, The Executions of the Third of May,* the *Majas,* and perhaps he had a glimpse of the "Black Paintings" in the Quinta del Sordo... But he had discovered Velázquez!

"The fine and the thick brushes with long stems," which Velázquez used, lengthen from century to century; they reach up to our own time: In Picasso's series "Las Meninas." The impression of a cinematic "freeze," produced by Velázquez' *Meninas*, dissolves and begins to move in Picasso's "Las Meninas" like a gigantic kaleidoscope... And, nevertheless, taken one by one, each of Picasso's "Meninas" tells us something more, distinctive and personal, something new, which is not yet to be found in Velázquez' *Meninas.* Or is it that they are both simply saying the same thing in different "languages"?

In any case, through Picasso's "Las Meninas," as if we were looking through a magic glass, we see something in Velázquez which we had not seen before. And the same happened in the mid-19th century with Manet's *Dejeuner sur l'herbe,* for example. And with many of Goya's paintings at the end of the 18th century... This crystal of several centuries, this glass of time (undoubtedly a magic magnifying glass) has revealed aspects of Velázquez which his contemporaries could not see, because they weren't prophets, although Palomino intuitively realised them; which were hidden for more than a century, until Goya; which dazzled Manet and which Picasso, the analytical Cubist, would analyse, "something" in Velázquez which—through the fault of Palomino!—we have called the great "truth": "It is truth, it is not painting," this intelligent and sensitive critic from Seville has been telling us since the 17th century! That is all very well, but what is that great "truth"? How are we to detect this great truth in Velázquez' work? Is it a moral precept which guides his art? Is it a pictorial technique, known only to Velázquez? Is it...?

I say sincerely: I wish I knew! Or rather: I wish I had discovered it! Or, still better: I wish I had invented it.

# APPENDIX

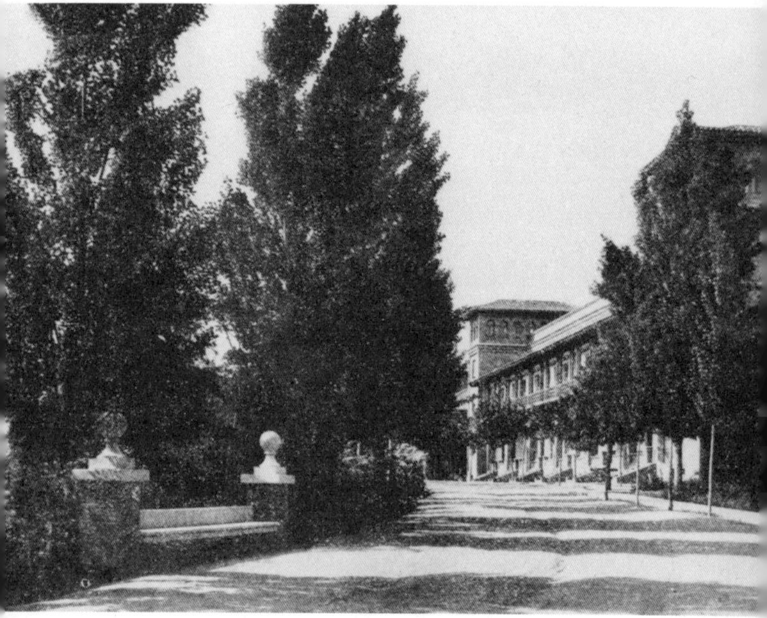

**Photograph of the Duke of Alba's bench (left) and the Pabellón Transatlántico (right) at the Residencia de Estudiantes, Madrid, 1920s.** (Residencia de Estudiantes, Madrid)

## THE DUKE OF ALBA'S BENCH, RESIDENCIA DE ESTUDIANTES, MADRID

The postcard headed, like a diplomatic visiting card with the initials "p.p.c." (pour prendre congé), to take leave (written in pencil of course), folded carelessly in half to indicate that it had been left personally at the door of its recipient by the sender, whose name should be embossed on the white cardboard... (Although, in fact, his chauffeur would have delivered it or, in earlier days, the footman who accompanied the chauffeur to open the car door for His Excellency when he got in or out). In any case, this is my card—postcard—"p.p.c." to take my leave of you who have arrived here in my company, page after page.

"Here" is the Duke of Alba's bench in the Residencia de Estudiantes, calle del Pinar, Madrid. That is to say, in the garden of the Residencia, facing the attractive brick pavilions with their white balconies and green shutters, designed by the architect Antonio Flores. The bench is brick and granite, finished off at each end by two granite balls, simple, sober, and magnificent, reminiscent of the Friars' Garden in El Escorial. But the garden they face is not that of Philip II's friars' but—with its trimmed box hedges, roses and oleanders—the garden planned, planted and tended by the poet Juan Ramón Jiménez in the 1920s. Because in those years—the twenties—the Residencia was the most important cultural and educational centre in Spain; much more important than the University of Madrid, which the resident students were attending, or the historic and illustrious University of Salamanca, whose rector in those days was Miguel de Unamuno.

Through the Residencia—through its conference hall (occasionally concert hall), its laboratories, its libraries and its garden—have passed the most outstanding personalities of the Europe of those years—now so distant—: From Paul Valéry to García Lorca, from Ramón y Cajal to Mme. Curie, from Ortega y Gasset to Count Keiserling (or vice versa), from H.G.Wells to Chesterton and from Unamuno to Baroja. It was in the Residencia that Lorca, Dalí and Buñuel, no less, coincided as young students and became friends. Lorca's piano still has its place in the salon ("the salon in the dark corner") of the "Resi."

The Residencia, which is now regaining the importance which was suppressed during the Franco era, was an official institution created by the Junta para Ampliación de Estudios (the Board for the Enlargement of Studies) in the Ministry of Public Education and Fine Art, a board which, in its own turn, was inspired by the Institución Libre de Enseñanza. My uncle, the eminent biologist, Antonio de Zulueta, had his small, Tolstoyan laboratory in the garden of the Residencia. As a child, I often went to play with my Zulueta cousins in the garden created by Juan Ramón Jiménez, a garden "for grown-ups" which delighted us. On some afternoons, hiding behind the hedges, we would watch with admiration a young student, in shorts and bare chested, who would spend hours hitting a leather ball, suspended from a kind of coat hanger. I say "with admiration" because the Residencia's porter, an old and good friend of ours, had told us that this student was the amateur boxing champion—flyweight, featherweight or whatever—of Spain. This amateur champion was Luis Buñuel; that is to say, he would become Buñuel. (I learned some years later, that the ants in *Un perro andaluz* had been captured in the garden of the Residencia and sent to Paris, where Buñuel was making the film, in a biscuit tin. Surrealist ants without a doubt.)

A flexible line of ants—not surrealist, perhaps a bit "pop," winds round one of the great stone balls on the bench where four friends are sitting, drinking and chatting before lunch. These are the Colombian poet and novelist, Álvaro Mutis, one of my oldest and best friends, his wife Carmen, Jacobo Fitz-James Stuart, Count of Siruela, the grandson of that Duke of Alba who had given the bench its name, and myself. It is a day in the year 1990, one of the last days of the Velázquez exhibition in the Prado, a rare day of tepid sunshine and a sky of faded blue, in a Spring marked by torrents of rain, without a glimpse of that blue Madrid sky which seems to have lost its transparency...

(Pollution?, humidity?, age? —one's own age—?)

I was telling them an anecdote from my adolescence, my first ——and, I think, only—visit to my father's government office when, in the Spring of 1934, he was Foreign Minister in the Republican Government, presided by Azaña. I told them how elegant the minister's office was then, in the charming old palace of Santa Cruz, brick and granite, like the bench where we were sitting, completed by two brick towers beneath pyramidal roofs of grey slate, and with an enormous escutcheon and crown of the Austrian rulers above the iron central balcony. But the office was modern, large and square, with a few heavy pieces of furniture, four-square and rectangular, of grey suede; grey walls covered in a heavy, opaque Chinese silk on which there stood out a single small picture, over an austere fireplace of polished granite: A Hieronymus Bosch! The ceiling was vaulted and white, the floor covered by an enormous Persian carpet in dark tones. My father told me that the room had been redecorated by Jacobo Fitz-James Stuart, Duke of Alba, the grandfather of Jacobo Fitz-James Stuart, Count of Siruela. The Duke was Foreign Minister in Alfonso XIII's last government, my father the second in the Spanish Republic.

And now we were here, Jacobo Fitz-James Stuart and Luis de Zulueta, both "junior" as the Americans would say, talking, naturally, about Velázquez. Jacobo Siruela, so precise in his judgements and exact in his images, said that he too had felt that impression produced by *Las Meninas* of a cinematic "freeze," which, when one turns one's back, will start to move again:

> It seems to me that the infanta Margarita is going to detach herself from the ground—her minute farthingale leaves a distinct shadow on the floor, as if she had already been lifted above the tiles of the gallery in the prince's quarters—and was starting to rise like a silk balloon, silently, to the mute astonishment of attendants, ladies in waiting, officers, dwarfs and dogs; and of the king and queen in the mirror... Because Velázquez alone knows what is happening. The silk balloon reaches the roof, passes through it like light through a crystal, rises and is lost, a tiny point of light in the clear sky... And then the blue sky, solitary, radiant, the glory of the Austrias.

And here below, in the Madrid of 1990, the long queues which wind round the *façade* of the Prado——often under umbrellas; *en abril, aguas mil*—. Hundreds of thousands, anxious to see and understand the new acquisition. Because Velázquez returned to life, or, more exactly, came into the world in Madrid, into the intricate world of communication which we suffer today, in that Spring of 1990. And he had died in Madrid more than three centuries earlier, in 1660. Velázquez: 1660-1990. A miracle!

THIS BOOK WAS PRINTED
IN MADRID, AUTUMN, 2006.
THREE AND A HALF CENTU-
RIES BEFORE, VELÁZQUEZ
PAINTED *LAS MENINAS*